HOLY FIRE

The Kingdom of God

BOOK THREE

HOLY FIRE

The Kingdom of God

DR. KEVIN L. ZADAI

Cover design: Virtually Possible Designs

Warrior Notes Publishing
P O Box 1288
Destrehan, LA 70047

For more information about our school, go to www.warriornotesschool.com. Reach us on the internet: www.Kevinzadai.com

ISBN 13 TP: 978-1-6631-0050-4

DEDICATION

I dedicate this book to the Lord Jesus Christ. When I died during surgery and met with Jesus on the other side, He insisted that I return to life on the earth and that I help people with their destinies. Because of Jesus's love and concern for people, the Lord has actually chosen to send a person back from death to help everyone who will receive that help so that his or her destiny and purpose are secure in Him.

I want You, Lord, to know that when You come to take me to be with You someday, I sincerely hope that people remember not me but the revelation of Jesus Christ that You have revealed through me. I want others to know that I am merely being obedient to Your Heavenly calling and mission, which is to reveal Your plan to fulfill the divine destiny for each of God's children.

ACKNOWLEDGMENTS

In addition to sharing my story with everyone through the book *Heavenly Visitation: A Guide to the Supernatural,* God has commissioned me to write over sixty books and study guides. Most recently, the Lord gave me the commission to produce the *Holy Fire* series. This book addresses some of the revelations concerning the areas that Jesus reviewed and revealed to me through the Word of God and by the Spirit of God during several visitations. I want to thank everyone who has encouraged me, assisted me, and prayed for me during the writing of this work. Special thanks to my wonderful wife, Kathi, for her love and dedication to the Lord and me. Thank you to a great staff for the wonderful job editing this book. Special thanks as well to all my friends who understand what it is to live in the holy fire of God and how to operate in this for the next move of God's Spirit.

CONTENTS

Salvation Prayer

INTRODUCTION

When Jesus visited me, He warned me that a season of testing was coming to earth and that many people were not ready due to their lukewarmness. Then I noticed that others were able to persevere in times of trouble and persecution. What was it that distinguished those who were prepared and those who were not? The answer is the baptism of the holy fire from the altar of God.

Jesus was the Son of Man, not just the Son of God, so His life, recorded in the Word of God, is an example to us. His life is written to help us to walk in the same fire of the Holy Spirit that He did. The baptism with holy fire paralyzes the devil and empowers you to function in your calling as a chosen one.

As you read this book, I pray that you will become more intimately acquainted with the Holy Spirit, who is a flame of fire, so that you may walk on the highway of holiness.

Blessings,
Dr. Kevin Zadai

1

TURN YOUR WEAKNESS INTO STRENGTH

And He said to me, "My grace is sufficient for you, for
My strength is made perfect in weakness."
—2 Corinthians 12:9

In the Old Testament, people were not led by the Holy Spirit like we are today because they did not have Him inside of them as we do. The Old Testament prophets and outward signs led them. The angel of the Lord led the Israelites in the desert, manifesting as a pillar of fire by night and a cloud by day (Exodus 13:21–22).

The Lord showed me that Joshua was constantly with Moses, and every time God had an opportunity to intervene, interject, or commune with Moses, Joshua was right there. When the tent of meeting was made and set up for all of Israel to seek the Lord, only Joshua and Moses entered and took advantage of it (Exodus 33:9–11). Joshua laid before the Lord continually, so can you guess who was chosen to take over for Moses—Joshua—and in his weakness, he became strong.

IN OUR WEAKNESS, THE SPIRIT OF GOD GIVES US POWER

Can you imagine spending time around Moses, witnessing everything happening with him, and thinking about the fact that the people did not want to engage with God? Moses was probably godly beyond what we could comprehend today, yet Joshua stayed there with him, and look what happened: Joshua became a mighty warrior.

As we see in the Bible, Joshua led Israel into the promised land, but he had to go and conquer all those cities first with the giants in them. In the cities of the land of Israel, like Jericho, vile, evil people had to be taken out. We often think of the weaknesses of an individual as a disadvantage. However, 2 Corinthians 12:9 teaches that in our weakness, the Spirit of God comes in and gives us strength.

*Likewise the Spirit also helps in our weaknesses. For
we do not know what we should pray for as we ought,
but the Spirit Himself makes intercession for us with
groanings which cannot be uttered.*

—Romans 8:26

The apostle Paul was a strong and hard-headed man; before he was saved, he persecuted and killed Christians. I think about how strong and well-learned Paul was and how he was being trained as an orator. He studied under Gamaliel, the head Pharisee. From what the writings say, Paul, who at that time was named Saul, was being prepared to take over as the head Pharisee (Acts 22:3–5). He was persecuting Christians to impress those in leadership so they would see how zealous he was. Of course, God intervened, and Saul was converted and changed his name to Paul (Acts 22:6–16).

THE DEEP MYSTERIES OF GOD ARE GIVEN TO US BY THE HOLY SPIRIT

*And I, brethren, when I came to you, did not come
with excellence of speech or of wisdom declaring to
you the testimony of God. For I determined not to
know anything among you except Jesus Christ and
Him crucified. I was with you in weakness, in fear,*

5

*and in much trembling. And my speech and my
preaching were not with persuasive words of human
wisdom, but in demonstration of the Spirit and of
power, that your faith should not be in the wisdom of
men but in the power of God.*

—1 Corinthians 2:1–5

After his conversion, Paul ministered in Corinth, a diverse and
cultural city that was wise in the wisdom of man. In this letter he
wrote to the Corinthians, Paul said he didn't come with enticing
words of man's wisdom but in demonstration of the Spirit and of
power (1 Corinthians 2:4). They might have thought that Paul would
come and be an orator because he was well-learned and trained.
Still, it says that Paul came with trembling. He was weak and only
proclaimed the revelation that Jesus gave him. He talked about this
wisdom given by God and how it is only spiritually discerned.

Paul told the people that "the Spirit searches all things, yes, the deep
things of God" (1 Corinthians 2:10–16). The wisdom of the ages,
the deep things of the Spirit, will be given to us by God, only from
Spirit to spirit. Paul explained that the deep mysteries had been
given to us through the Holy Spirit; the Spirit knows the mind of
God and reveals it to us. Then he said, "But we have the mind of
Christ" (1 Corinthians 2:16). Paul was no longer claiming to be

strong in himself. What happened to change his personality? Paul realized that all that learning had not gotten him anywhere because he was on his way to hell.

The Pharisees were promoting a religion that put bondages on people. Jesus said that the Pharisees were supposed to be taking yokes off people, but instead, they were putting them on people (Matthew 23:4–5). Jesus strongly rebuked the Pharisees, calling them a brood of vipers (Matthew 3:7). Paul was humbled after he had a visitation from Jesus Himself, Who taught him about the gospel message that he would soon preach.

Amazingly, no man taught Paul the gospel. When you read his letters, Paul has extraordinary insight into what we have obtained through Jesus Christ, which was all received by revelation. In the books of Ephesians and Colossians, we see that we have been seated with Christ in the heavenly realms (Ephesians 2:6, Colossians 3:1). Throughout his writings, Paul explains that we have been given authority and the ability to understand the mystery of the ages about the church. He shares powerful insights about the body of Christ, the gifts of the Holy Spirit, and the fivefold ministry of the church. Paul revealed these secrets to the New Testament church and us.

Paul disappeared from the scene for several years, then reappeared with this gospel message. We have all this revelation from Paul, which he received in his deep, intimate time with the Lord. He was caught up in Heaven and was speaking from the heavenly realm. In the same way, Joshua was prepared by the Lord. We can see this when he encountered the angel of the Lord on the way up to Jericho (Joshua 5:13–15). He met the Commander of the Lord's army, and God showed him that an army of angels was working with him the whole time.

GOD'S STRENGTH IS SHOWN IN OUR WEAKNESS

And He said to me, "My grace is sufficient for you, for My strength is made perfect in weakness." Therefore most gladly I will rather boast in my infirmities, that the power of Christ may rest upon me. Therefore I take pleasure in infirmities, in reproaches, in needs, in persecutions, in distresses, for Christ's sake. For when I am weak, then I am strong.

2 Corinthians 12:9–10

Paul was very weak and humble, yet look at what he did. He told us that weakness was actually where God's strength was shown. He gloried in his weaknesses because that is where the power of God is

8

revealed. You are being set up when your weaknesses are exposed because you still have to function in this realm. You will not cease to be who you are just because you fail, situations don't work out, or you sometimes feel like you cannot go on. The Spirit of God comes in at those times and wants to be a Comforter (John 14:26).

Even Joshua must have felt weak, always following Moses around. Moses was probably an intense person because of what he experienced on the mountain with God and with those angels around him. The first five books of the Bible were dictated to Moses. He wrote the Pentateuch, including Genesis, which was given to him verbatim—think about that. Moses was not even alive during Genesis, yet he wrote it. Now, how did he do that? The angels dictated to him.

Moses was given the law and all the instructions from God. He saw the glory of God and encountered that glory realm for days at a time. Joshua emerged from that environment as a leader. In Joshua's weakness, as he laid before the Lord, he was formed into who God called him to be.

But when God, Who had chosen me and set me apart
before I was born, and called me through His grace,
was pleased to reveal His Son in me so that I might

*preach Him among the Gentiles [as the good news—
the way of salvation], I did not immediately consult
with anyone [for guidance regarding God's call and
His revelation to me]. Nor did I [even] go up to
Jerusalem to those who were apostles before me; but
I went to Arabia and stayed awhile, and afterward
returned once more to Damascus.*

—Galatians 1:15–17 AMP

Saul, who became Paul, was humbled and brought into the
revelation of the gospel. Jesus caught him up to Heaven, and then
he disappeared for years. During that time, Paul knew that God's
strength was his friend. Paul said that when he was weak, he was
made strong because the Lord revealed His strength through his
weakness.

THE LORD STARTED YOUR FAITH,
AND HE WILL FINISH IT

*Therefore we also, since we are surrounded by so
great a cloud of witnesses, let us lay aside every
weight, and the sin which so easily ensnares us, and
let us run with endurance the race that is set before
us, looking unto Jesus, the author and finisher of our*

faith, Who for the joy that was set before Him endured the cross, despising the shame, and has sat down at the right hand of the throne of God.

—Hebrews 12:1–2

Remember that whatever you are going through is a divine setup. You must look at it that way. I notice that when I start to feel weak in any way, I am about to take a step into the supernatural. The Lord is your Commander. He has begun your faith and will finish it; He knows how to set you up and make you strong. The Lord will reveal your weaknesses only to have you rely on Him, which is what took place in the lives of both Joshua and Paul.

> *I notice that when I start to feel weak in any way, I am about to take a step into the supernatural.*

When Joshua and Caleb came back from spying out the promised land, Caleb said, "Let us go up at once and take possession, for we are well able to overcome it" (Numbers 13:30). They were young, yet they had it within them to see God be faithful to their generation. They knew they could take the giants (Numbers 14:6–9). Unfortunately, the whole generation, except for them, doubted God and fell in the desert. They were all supposed to enter the promised land, but Joshua and Caleb had to wait forty years.

IT IS UP TO YOU TO KEEP YOURSELF SPIRITUALLY HOT

Moses lived in the courts of Pharaoh until he was forty years old, then he had to flee and spend another forty years in the Midian Desert. Likewise, the children of Israel spent forty years in the desert, and then they all fell. The next generation entered the promised land. In our human frailty, we seem to become lukewarm.

We find ourselves in situations where we are promised so many blessings, and God is willing and ready, yet just a few people are prepared to go. The rest of the people seem to drag their feet. I am always amazed because I see this happen all the time. All of God's people suffer the consequences of lukewarmness, both those who are willing to do what God has for them, along with those who do not. Some churches resist the move of God, which you see throughout church history.

The demonic forces in the world want to wear you out, especially when you are willing and ready to go forth with God. You need to get other people on board with you. They need to learn spiritual warfare so that you all can bind and loose, waging good warfare in your territory (Matthew 16:19; 1 Timothy 1:18). Sometimes it is up to individuals to work with the Holy Spirit to bring about a move of God, even if it starts in a smaller group of people. In our weaknesses, God is revealed to be strong. Sometimes, regional breakthrough comes through small gatherings of people who meet; they become the remnant.

Sometimes you need to get away from a stiff-necked group, which is why people leave churches. People often want to go on with God, but their group does not, so they leave and join others who are hungry for God. Throughout history, God moved, and people moved with Him, causing His movement to grow. However, after a while, many seemed to grow cold. Then another group of people, a remnant, will emerge, and another movement will start. Throughout the years, I have studied church history and seen this cycle happen many times.

I formed Warrior Notes, the Warrior Fellowship Churches worldwide, the school, and everything we do at Warrior Notes for one reason: to stop the cycle of lukewarmness in the church. We see a remnant that wants to be hot again for the Lord, which is why we have the teaching on holy fire.

God wants us always to have that fire burning in our lives; that way, we will never grow cold. We should never have to have revival again because we are alive in Christ. We never have to have another move of God because God is constantly moving. We are called to remain hot, perpetually encountering the fire of God.

> *Having disarmed principalities and powers, He made a public spectacle of them, triumphing over them in it.*
>
> —Colossians 2:15

Paul made certain statements from his revelations that really should keep us hot. He was not a cold or lukewarm Christian and was adamant about what the Lord told him. One of the things he said that was very profound to me is in Colossians 2:15, which speaks of Jesus's triumph over the enemy. I have noticed in Christianity that groups of people and individuals are unaware or may have let it slip away from them. This truth may be mentioned, but it is not emphasized.

It is up to us to emphasize the truth and keep ourselves individually hot. Our spiritual temperature will cool down unless we each take action to keep it hot. Often, the church or ministry groups we are involved with are attacked by the enemy, their fire goes out, and they become lukewarm, so they no longer grow. Your spirit will no longer thrive in these groups. They do not get together to pray, intercede, or pull down strongholds. They do not proclaim what God has for the region and their nation.

NO MATTER WHAT DEMONIC ENTITY WE ENCOUNTER, JESUS HAS DISARMED THEM

Since we go through these cycles, we must understand and be reminded that Jesus already disarmed our enemy. If we feel weak and encounter demonic strongholds, we must remember that Jesus has disarmed them, no matter what demonic entity we face.

> *For we do not wrestle against flesh and blood, but against principalities, against powers, against the rulers of the darkness of this age, against spiritual hosts of wickedness in the heavenly places.*
>
> —Ephesians 6:12

Jesus has disarmed the principalities and powers, which are the four divisions of spiritual forces Paul lists in Ephesians. Paul mentions that Jesus made a public spectacle of them and triumphed over them, which means that He embarrassed them publicly (Colossians 2:15). What does that mean?

Think about where you are and where the church is. Then look at yourself in three periods: before you knew Christ, since you have known Christ, and in the future. What do you want to look like, and where are you going? Hopefully, you want to go into a fiery move of God.

If you want to dwell in a hot furnace with the flames of the Holy Spirit, you must understand some established truths that are not being emphasized at all. Jesus destroyed the works of the devil. He literally took their weapons away from them, which is what we should see when we encounter the enemy; they must lie down and listen to what we say. The enemy should be moving out of the way. If they are not, we may have to pray in groups of people or have the body of Christ as a whole address certain levels of demonic activity. Some things have to be done corporately.

> *You must remind the demons that they are defeated and drive them out because they hope you forget to enforce it.*

When dealing with a nation like the United States, you will need the corporate church to come in unity against certain territorial spirits, or the enemy will succeed in stealing, killing, and destroying. If we are not careful, the demonic spirits even try to use people above us in leadership positions. If the church is compromised, these demonic spirits also influence those people. Even though Christians cannot be demon-possessed, they can certainly be influenced by the spirit of the air. Peter was influenced in that way (Matthew 16:23).

If demons are attacking or influencing our lives, we must reinforce the victory of Jesus Christ, which has already been addressed in the Word of God. You must remind the demons that they are defeated and drive them out because they hope you forget to enforce it. The Bible has a lot of truth, but it is not being taught. As a result, we are seeing many people who are weak when they should be strong. If they knew some of these truths, they would manifest that strength.

JESUS WAS MANIFESTED TO DESTROY THE WORKS OF THE DEVIL

He who sins is of the devil, for the devil has sinned from the beginning. For this purpose the Son of God was manifested, that He might destroy the works of the devil.

—1 John 3:8

How God anointed Jesus of Nazareth with the Holy Spirit and with power, Who went about doing good and healing all who were oppressed by the devil, for God was with Him.

—Acts 10:38

Here is another truth from the Word of God: The devil sins and has been sinning from the beginning; for this purpose, the Son of God, Jesus, was manifested that He might destroy the works of the devil. Jesus went around doing good and healing all who were oppressed by the devil. As He was manifested, He undid the works of the devil. He started to make people healthy again when they were sick. Jesus was doing good. So God is a good God Who sent Jesus to do good works. And these are all established truths.

The verses we just studied—Colossians 2:15; Ephesians 6:12; 1 John 3:8; and Acts 10:38—are essential to learn so you will not have a deficit. You must be able to deal with situations based on truth, but you can't do that if you are unaware of the truth. If you have heard these Scriptures before but don't keep them before you, you are not walking in that truth, which will hurt you. If someone knows the truth and walks in it, it is evident because there is fruit. If someone knows the truth but does not walk in it, it is just as bad as not understanding it. Either way, the result is the same. You have no fruit being manifested.

Jesus came to the world, was manifested, destroyed the works of the devil, and went around doing good and healing everyone. That is what we are called to do too. The devil has all these plans, yet Paul said that we are not ignorant of the enemy's battle strategies or his *devices,* which is what 2 Corinthians 2:11 says in the King James Version. Jesus undid and destroyed the plans and strategies of the enemy, which is essential information. If Paul said we are not ignorant of satan's devices, I would think *I need to know that.*

Years ago, when I didn't know satan's battle strategies, I asked the Lord for insight. Why is the devil allowed to work in a Christian's life if he has been disarmed? Why is he allowed to go around doing evil? Why aren't Christians going around doing good and healing everyone who is oppressed by the devil as Jesus did? I didn't know or understand these truths then and thought there was either a lack of knowledge or implementation, resulting in no manifestation.

The Lord revealed to me that in our weakness, He comes in His strength and girds us up so that we see His power in that weakness. As Christians, we must enforce our victory and forbid the devil to get away with his attacks. Christians are able to do what Jesus did. I want to see the manifestation of the power of God, which has to do with managing our weaknesses and allowing the Holy Spirit to come in and be our strength.

2

THE DEVIL CAN HAVE NOTHING IN YOU

I will no longer talk much with you, for the ruler of this world is coming, and he has nothing in Me.
—John 14:30

Many Christians exhibit weaknesses, but they are not experiencing the power or the strength of the Holy Spirit coming in. It is one thing to feel weak, but it is another to let the Holy Spirit come in and do a supernatural work in your life to strengthen you. I do not want religion to keep people weak, which the Pharisees did. They wanted people to stay in weakness and be enslaved in bondage. Jesus told the Pharisees that they were supposed to be taking yokes off people, which is what we want to do through Warrior Notes ministry. We train you to set people free.

When people think they are holy because they are suffering, poor, or sick, it can be a religious mentality, a victim mentality, or something similar. In contrast, the gospel is against all oppression and bondage; it is good news that brings healing, strength, deliverance, jubilee, debt cancellation, and forgiveness of sins. Not only does the gospel bring the good news of forgiveness of sin, but it also cleanses people from sin-consciousness. However, if you stay in a place of weakness and do not invite the Holy Spirit to strengthen you, you will remain weak, which is not pleasing to God.

EATING THE GOOD OF THE LAND

If you are willing and obedient, you shall eat the good of the land.

—Isaiah 1:19

Some people have this religious idea that God is making them sick because He wants to teach them something. Or they think that God wants them poor to humble them, but that is not how God works. God has already established His ways in the Word of God. God wants to prosper you because He said if you do all these things, you will have so much that you will lend to many, but you will not have to borrow, which sounds like prosperity to me (Deuteronomy 28:1–14). God promised He would take sickness from the midst of you, and you will not have to get sick anymore.

Do you remember how the Israelite's clothes and shoes never even wore out in the desert (Deuteronomy 29:5)? They were also supernaturally provided with manna and water and never got sick (Exodus 15:22–16:36). All these things were part of the covenant and promises of God. Although you cannot remain in your weakness, even so, weakness is your friend. Paul said that he gloried in his weaknesses because that was when the power of God was revealed (2 Corinthians 12:9). However, you have to go to that next step where God comes in and girds you up. That is when the Holy Spirit comforts you, brings resolution, and provides for you.

DO NOT LEAVE IT UP TO CHANCE

When you think about the world in its fallen state, it seems that if you let things go, they worsen; they do not fix themselves. We might straighten and clean up the house, but because of the fall, it gets dirty again; everything tends toward chaos. You organize your home, but everything seems to soon be in disarray again. Your house doesn't clean or straighten itself up or stay in order. If you let stuff go, it goes into chaos.

In the law of random chance with two choices, you have a fifty-fifty chance because there is only one answer or the other. If you leave it up to randomness, you should have a 50 percent chance of getting it right, so how could you fail 75 percent of the time? In this fallen world, when Christians rely on randomness, they allow evil spirits to come in, giving them a 100 percent chance of losing. Even though it would not be mathematically possible to lose that many times in a row, they do. If you flip a coin and say heads or tails, you have a fifty-fifty chance because there are only two choices, so if you do it four times in a row and miss it four times, at that point, something suspicious is happening. Evil spirits can supernaturally manipulate a Christian who lives by gambling or randomness, and you do not want to live like that.

LED BY THE HOLY SPIRIT

I will not be a slave to randomness because it is not in my favor. However, what *is* rigged in my favor is if I trust in God and the Holy Spirit leads me. The Holy Spirit can turn everything in my favor so that it is no longer random. That is better than fifty-fifty because you can win every time. If the Lord leads you, He will guide you into

His favor, not randomness; it is not like you are flipping a coin because the Spirit is leading you. The Holy Spirit is the Spirit of Truth, Who will lead you into all truth (John 16:13). That means you win, which is a higher law than randomness.

In the New Testament, when Judas hung himself, he was disqualified as one of the twelve and had to be replaced (Matthew 27:3–5). However, it does not say the Lord told them to choose another disciple or apostle. But they decided to follow an Old Testament practice and cast lots for who would replace Judas; they chose Mathias (Acts 1:26). In the New Testament, the Spirit of God is poured out. Now the Holy Spirit leads us. We are not led by prophets, the throwing of dice, or randomness—we are guided by the Spirit. The Holy Spirit inside each believer is doing away with chance and randomness.

The devil wants a Christian to operate in randomness or chance because he can get in there and cause trouble. However, the devil cannot manipulate the outcome if the Holy Spirit leads you. The Holy Spirit will always be correct and lead you to all truth. Now, the devil can steal that truth from you. The Holy Spirit could tell you the will of God, but it doesn't happen when evil spirits are allowed in to steal and take it away. That is what happened in the garden. God made the world and Adam and Eve perfect. Everything was fine, but the devil came in and stole people from God (Genesis 3). God permitted this to happen because we have free will. We see so many things like that happening today.

We do not want to be like the disciples who rolled the dice to choose the next person to replace Judas because God had already chosen each of them. In the Bible, Jesus did not roll dice to choose the disciples. He went up to the mountain and prayed all night, and God gave him the names of all His disciples in prayer (Luke 6:12–17). Jesus was led by the Spirit and chose the disciples.

So why were they rolling the dice and casting lots to select Judas's replacement? They ended up choosing Matthias, who is never heard of again in Scripture. It was never recorded that he did anything. That does not mean he didn't, but there is no record of him. However, there was a replacement for him—the one who announced that he was called to be an apostle from birth—Paul (Galatians 1:15–16). Paul was chosen to replace Judas, yet he came in another way. He became the apostle Paul, who did many great works for God and bore good fruit.

I do not make decisions by randomness or putting out fleeces as Gideon did (Judges 6:36–40). He put out a fleece, but that was in the Old Testament. Back then, they did not have the Holy Spirit inside them as we do. They did not have the gift of praying in tongues and all the resources we have today as believers. We have that intimate relationship with God. So in our weaknesses, we do not rely on astrology, tarot cards, or dice, and we do not get our income from gambling. We do not throw ourselves into situations with a fifty-fifty chance of winning. We do not do these random things because it is not of God. That is why we are forbidden to go to mediums, witches, or chart the stars.

> *There shall not be found among you anyone who makes his son or his daughter pass through the fire, or one who practices witchcraft, or a soothsayer, or one who interprets omens, or a sorcerer, or one who conjures spells, or a medium, or a spiritist, or one who calls up the dead. For all who do these things are an abomination to the Lord, and because of these abominations the Lord your God drives them out from before you.*
>
> —Deuteronomy 18:10–12

All these demonic activities listed in this passage are opposed to God's intimate relationship with us as believers. These practices are fueled by evil spirits, which is why you do not want to put out a fleece. You do not want to say, "If it is God's will, this or that will happen," because those evil spirits will hear what you say and go do it. Do not get into deception, be seduced, and drawn away by evil spirits by getting into wrong practices. Don't put yourself in a situation where the outcome is random.

You do not want to make decisions based on chance because it is not even a genuine chance—it is rigged. These evil spirits can rig situations against you, which you need to avoid. So do not involve yourself in those evil practices previously mentioned. Instead, place yourself in a situation where you seek God, petition the Lord in prayer, and have a 100 percent chance of getting your answer (Philippians 4:6–7). It is not random; it is *on purpose* because it is rigged in your favor by your Heavenly Father (Psalm 139:16).

RENEWED BY THE WORD OF GOD

I beseech you therefore, brethren, by the mercies of God, that you present your bodies a living sacrifice, holy, acceptable to God, which is your reasonable service. And do not be conformed to this world, but be transformed by the renewing of your mind, that you may prove what is that good and acceptable and perfect will of God.

—Romans 12:1–2

When you are born again, your spirit is redeemed, but your mind, will, and emotions are not. You must renew them by the Word of God. You must commit yourself to prayer, place your body on the altar as a living sacrifice, then deal with your soul and body individually as the Word of God says. You renew your mind, discipline your body, and build up your spirit by praying in the Holy Spirit and meditating on the Word of God (1 Corinthians 9:24–27; Romans 10:17; Jude 1:20).

God leads you in your spirit, not in your head or body. God took hold of your spirit when you were born again. He is not using outside forces to lead you because He can speak to your spirit. When the Holy Spirit baptized you, He got ahold of your tongue to control it. James said that if you have control over your tongue, you have control over your whole life (James 3:1–11). When the Holy Spirit controls your tongue, then when you pray in the Holy Spirit, you are led by the Holy Spirit.

THE SPIRIT PUTS TO DEATH THE MISDEEDS
OF THE BODY

I love God's law with all my heart. But there is another power within me that is at war with my mind.

This power makes me a slave to the sin that is still within me.

—Romans 7:22–23 NLT

Here, Paul is talking about his struggle with being under the religious system. Paul says he knew and loved the law, but another power made him a slave to sin. He could not accomplish what he wanted to do and found himself doing the opposite—doing things he did not want to do. Paul was distraught in Romans 7 because of this, but at the end of the chapter going into chapter 8, he thanked God that the answer is Jesus Christ our Lord! Living in the power of the Holy Spirit puts to death the misdeeds of the body (Romans 8:13).

So now there is no condemnation for those who belong to Christ Jesus. And because you belong to him, the power of the life-giving Spirit has freed you from the power of sin that leads to death.

—Romans 8:1–2 NLT

In Romans 7 and 8, Paul shows us that we can now overcome our weakness through the Spirit's power, but we must engage actively. It is not enough to say, "Well, I'm going to struggle like Romans 7 talks about, and God is being glorified because I'm weak." When you do that, you are glorifying your weakness without any

resolution. In Romans 8, we find out that we are supposed to be
walking in the Spirit, which puts to death the misdeeds of the body.

> *I look within my heart as I pray in the Spirit,*
> *and I see that my spirit lights up inside me.*

As a born-again Christian, I resolved within myself that I have the
power to put to death the misdeeds of the body. I also have the
ability to correct my thinking and have the mind of the Spirit and
not the mind of the flesh. I make that resolution within myself every
day.

I look within my heart as I pray in the Spirit, and I see that my spirit
lights up inside me. My mind is not fruitful when I pray in tongues,
but the Holy Spirit is in operation. I cannot comprehend what I am
saying because my spirit is talking to God, He speaks mysteries, and
I yield to that (1 Corinthians 14:2). I can see that power within me,
and then I know I can take that part of me and rule and reign in that
place.

> *For though we walk in the flesh, we do not war*
> *according to the flesh. For the weapons of our*

warfare are not carnal but mighty in God for pulling down strongholds, casting down arguments and every high thing that exalts itself against the knowledge of God, bringing every thought into captivity to the obedience of Christ, and being ready to punish all disobedience when your obedience is fulfilled.

—2 Corinthians 10:3–6

I will not yield to the flesh and be called carnal as Paul described the Corinthians (1 Corinthians 3:1). I will cast down any thought or anything that exalts itself above the knowledge of God and bring it into captivity to the obedience of Christ. I will take it by force, arrest it, throw it down, handcuff it, and incarcerate it. I will not allow anything that exalts itself above the knowledge of God to rule and reign in my life.

In 2 Corinthians, Paul talks about the weapons of our warfare not being carnal but mighty through God, and he uses very strong language. I am taking my spiritual life to where the strength is. And even when I am experiencing weakness in my flesh and mind, I use my spirit to rule and reign. I am taking every thought captive to the obedience of Christ. I am causing my flesh to be put under submission because the Holy Spirit and the power of God ignite a stronger part of me.

THE WAR WITHIN

There are three parts to us—spirit, soul, and body—but only one part is redeemed: your spirit. Your soul is being renewed by the Word of God, so it is in the process of being saved, healed, and delivered. We go through a journey and a process in this life. As Christians start to understand this, they are healed and delivered, and you can see it happening.

Many Christians are wrestling with issues, but the problem is they are not wrestling with devils all the time—they are wrestling with problems within themselves. Sometimes they are torn between two opinions and oscillate back and forth. They have hurt, unforgiveness, and all these sins they are dealing with in their soul that Jesus said are bad for your soil (Matthew 13:1–23). Jesus noted how important it was to remove these hindrances or else you would not have a crop.

I always think about how I must deal with my soul and soil. One way is by asking myself, *Why am I responding this way? Why do I think this way?* Then I take what is in the Word of God with the power of the Holy Spirit, and I arrest these false ideas. I take them captive and incarcerate them so they can never exist again. I have to correct them, and then I put to death the misdeeds of the body.

> *To be good at spiritual warfare, you must start with the war within you.*

Whenever my body wants to act up, I say *no* from my spirit; as my mind starts to side with my spirit, I become stronger. As you practice this as Christians and warriors, you will begin to see this happen with yourself and others. You will start to excel to the place where you walk in dominion. That means you will have control from your spirit over your mind and body. As your mind is renewed and sides with your spirit, you will see yourself and others escape the corruption that is in the world because you have become partakers of the divine nature (2 Peter 1:4). The divine nature is inside your spirit. Still, your mind has to be renewed or else it will side with your flesh, which is where the battle is going on.

To be good at spiritual warfare, you must start with the war within you. Are you halting between two opinions? Are you oscillating? Are you struggling with unbelief, fear, doubt, and all these different areas that need healing due to traumatic events? Are you taken with the cares of this life? Or are you tempted by money so that you love and want to chase after wealth? Do you want recognition and have issues with pride? You need to deal with these struggles within you because Jesus said these problems in the soil would lead to no harvest whatsoever. The seed does not take root in three of the four soils Jesus mentioned in Matthew 13.

If your heart is hard, you need it softened, and if you need to be forgiven, you need to forgive. You must get the rocks and the thorns out of your soil, which needs to be soft and broken up. You need to be healed within you so that the battle is gone. Once you get all that out, you can discover how to engage in spiritual warfare with territories and all that entails.

> *I will not speak with you much longer, for the ruler of the world (satan) is coming. And he has no claim on Me [no power over Me nor anything that he can use against Me]; but so that the world may know [without any doubt] that I love the Father, I do exactly as the Father has commanded Me [and act in full agreement with Him].*
>
> —John 14:30–31 AMP

It comes down to this—when the devil comes, does he have something in you? In John 14:30–31, Jesus said that satan had no claim on Him; he had no power over Him or anything he could use against Him. Real warfare starts when the devil comes and tries to get you to fight yourself within yourself.

That happened to Peter. He was fine walking to Jesus on the water until he looked at his circumstances and started to waver (Matthew 14:22–33). He was dealing with issues going on within him that needed to be healed. Jesus told Peter that when he repented and turned, he would minister to the brethren (Luke 22:31–32). After the resurrection, Jesus met with Peter, and everything was restored, but this process must also happen with us (John 21:14–19).

We cannot stay in our weaknesses. Weakness is meant to reveal God's strength so we don't live there. We don't make a monument, a temple, or a denomination over it. We go on to resolve it in the power of God. The power of God must be revealed in our weakness, or we have not completed the whole process. Make sure you list what you are dealing with and need to take care of because I want you to be healed. You must eliminate the rocks, thorns, and hard soil within you so it can be perfect for producing a crop.

Prayer:

I ask You, Lord God, to remove those things from us, whatever is in our soil, in our souls, that is hindering us. Clean up our soil so that it is perfect, and we can produce a crop of thirtyfold, sixtyfold, and one hundredfold. In Jesus's name, Amen.

3

RESOLUTION AND PROVISION

Now faith is the substance of things hoped for, the
evidence of things not seen.
—Hebrews 11:1

There are works of the Spirit and works of the flesh. However, not everyone knows witchcraft is listed in Scripture as a work of the flesh. We seem to think that witchcraft is part of spiritual warfare. The demons are spirits, but they attach themselves to people in their souls, and they get witches and warlocks to side with them and use them. The demons hijack them to use them in the soul realm, then manifest through them in the flesh.

The demons want to express themselves in this realm because they are disembodied. They hijack people by intermixing themselves into their emotions and their wills. Then they can use people as guided missiles or puppets, which happened with Peter when Jesus rebuked him for speaking on satan's behalf. Jesus actually said to Peter, "Get behind Me, satan! You are an offense to Me, for you are not mindful of the things of God, but the things of men" (Matthew 16:23). Jesus talked to Peter as though he were satan himself. Peter was setting an example there to show that even believing Christians could be used to think and say the wrong thing.

> *Now the works of the flesh are manifest, which are these; adultery, fornication, uncleanness, lasciviousness, idolatry, witchcraft, hatred, variance, emulations, wrath, strife, seditions, heresies, envyings, murders, drunkenness, revellings, and such like: of the which I tell you before, as I have also told you in time past, that they which do such things shall not inherit the kingdom of God.*
>
> —Galatians 5:19–21 KJV

Galatians lists the works or the manifestations of the flesh, one of which is sorcery or witchcraft. You might think this is a spiritual problem, but here, Paul is talking about the manifestation of the spirit behind it. He says that the works of the flesh are evident. Paul is talking about evil spirits behind these works, manipulating people to manifest these sins. Paul said that you would not inherit the kingdom of God if you manifest these sins.

THE MANIFESTATIONS OF THE HOLY SPIRIT ARE THE FRUIT OF THE SPIRIT

So if you actively and consistently engage in these works of the flesh, you manifest the wrong spirit. You are manifesting the works of the devil through your own flesh. When you continually engage in these things, God cannot allow you into His kingdom. The manifestations of the Spirit are the fruit of the Spirit, which are all the opposite of what is being said here (Galatians 5:22–23).

Witchcraft is a work of the flesh, even though evil spirits have an influence. Paul said, "The weapons of our warfare are not carnal but mighty in God for pulling down strongholds, casting down arguments and every high thing that exalts itself against the knowledge of God, bringing every thought into captivity to the obedience of Christ" (2 Corinthians 10:4–5). This passage teaches about spiritual warfare on the highest level, yet it talks about dealing with thoughts in our minds, which is the psychological realm.

Paul says that we are dealing with manifestations of evil spirits in the flesh, and then he lists the works of the flesh. These works are essentially the evil spirits promoting their doctrine through a manifestation in people's flesh. I understand everything originates within the spirit realm because that was the first realm. Sometimes to explain a person's behavior, we say it is just how they are. However, if you looked into it, you would find that the root and origin of their behavior was sin. In the same way, the root and origin of the disease was sin, which had to do with the devil because he was sinning from the beginning (1 John 3:8).

THE DEVIL IS BEHIND SICKNESS, POVERTY, AND EVERY CURSE AND SIN

How God anointed Jesus of Nazareth with the Holy Spirit and with power, Who went about doing good and healing all who were oppressed by the devil, for God was with Him.

—Acts 10:38

Jesus went around doing good and healing everyone oppressed by the devil. Right there, Acts 10:38 says that the sickness that Jesus was healing was from oppression by the devil. Everything has a spiritual origin. When you investigate someone, you find out it is not just about them; they somehow picked up that affliction from this fallen world. You will find the devil behind sickness, poverty, and every curse and sin. The devil is enforcing some traits and sins handed down through generations (Exodus 20:5). These evil spirits enforce the curse, and you will find those traits replicated in the next generation, and you wonder how that happened.

When someone dies, the evil spirits assigned to them don't die; they are just transferred. They live in a territory and follow family bloodlines. They stay in an area, enforcing what they are assigned to do. I have found that when you investigate why certain people are the way they are, the devil is somehow behind it, because he is enforcing the curse on this fallen world. In the same way, Heaven's angels are assigned to specific areas and individuals to implement their assignment. These angels provide security, but more than that, they enforce the blessing and the covenant and do God's bidding.

The devil wants to extinguish the human race and ensure that nobody goes to Heaven. He is so angry at God that he is not satisfied with the separation of people from God; he wants to destroy the human race. He wants to make it hard for us and torment us. Still, Jesus came back and destroyed the works of the devil (1 John 3:8). We cannot stay in our weakness very long because God's resurrection power has to come in, and the Holy Spirit wants to reaffirm that Jesus has conquered the devil and that He is healing.

When someone wants me to pray for them, I need to hear a brief explanation of what is going on. I want to know what I have to go after because I will take back what the devil stole from them. That is what Jesus did. He had compassion for people but wanted to correct what was wrong; He was restoring the kingdom for His Father. Jesus went around doing good and healing everyone. When ministering healing, you cannot glorify what the devil is doing. First, you must identify that it is the devil and what is happening. Then you connect with your Heavenly Father and transfer what God is doing by the laying on of hands. You pray and see God's will done.

> *For the word of God is living and powerful, and sharper than any two-edged sword, piercing even to the division of soul and spirit, and of joints and marrow, and is a discerner of the thoughts and intents of the heart.*
>
> —Hebrews 4:12

Hebrews 4:12 describes the Lord coming in with His word, discerning and separating, dividing the soul and spirit. At some point, God brings a resolution when He comes. You do not want to keep glorifying the devil and focusing on what he is doing. You want to discern what is of the devil and what is of God, and then you want to go right after what God is doing. God distinguishes between the soul and spirit not just to show you but because He wants resolution. At some point, you take care of what is of the soul; you cannot just stay stuck in your problem.

> *The Lord can define a situation through separation with the sword of the Spirit, but then you have to move forward into deliverance and healing.*

You must not continue sharing with people that you are sick, repeating all your symptoms and what you go through daily. The only way to take care of it would be to discern what is of the spirit, what is of the soul, and what is going on in your body. Then resolution must come, which is what ministry is all about; it is not focusing on the weakness. Ministry focuses on the solution or the strength of God. The Lord can define a situation through the separation with the sword of the Spirit, but then you have to move forward into deliverance and healing. There must be resolution and provision.

Ministry is not always about wrestling with demons. Sometimes, you are dealing with people's souls, which are just as real, even though they might not manifest demons. You can hear what they say or see how they act. A person does not have to be completely taken over to be influenced by a demon. You may realize that someone is deceived by listening to what they say, because what they say will reveal what is in their heart (Matthew 12:36).

In deliverance, people aren't generally thrown on the ground, spitting up, and speaking profanity, even though that sometimes happens. In most deliverances, people just feel something leave them. Often, they sense the demon leave that oppressed their mind, will, and emotions, or when they feel something leave their body, they have a manifestation of healing. Manifestations will differ because evil spirits have different degrees of how they influence people.

Not everyone is possessed. Christians cannot even be possessed because the blood of Jesus has purchased them, but they may need to be delivered in their soul (Galatians 3:13–15). An evil spirit may influence them, so they have problems in their minds, emotions, or wills. That is why I like to know what is happening with someone. Suppose someone has a characteristic or personal trait that does not align with being an imitator of God as a dearly beloved child

(Ephesians 5:1–2). In this case, they are not manifesting the fruit of the Spirit. That is how you know that there needs to be transformation and resolution.

First, people must understand that there is a problem and a discrepancy. Then you have to call their situation as it is. If a person's life doesn't align with the checklist of the fruit of the Spirit and if there are manifestations of lying, cheating, sorcery, adultery, or any work of the flesh, then you have to label that (Galatians 5:19–21). If you observe love, peace, joy, and the consideration of others more than the consideration of self, then you know that God's Spirit is manifesting in that person (Galatians 5:22–23).

For example, if someone is always late and cannot be on time, they are being inconsiderate of other people's schedules. It is chronic. A spirit is trying to cause others to see them in a bad light. If that person finds it hard to be on time, they must overcome this. I watched this happen with others and have seen many friends fired from our previous employment. Our job required us not only to be on time but to be ten minutes early. Even though it was one of the best-paying jobs you could have, people could not seem to overcome something that was constantly working against them. These evil spirits will try to trip you up and ruin your momentum so you cannot do what you want.

One area that demons use to trip up people involves keeping their word. In the past, many good Christian friends lost their jobs where I worked. They were solid people who were supposed to have those jobs but lost them because they could not show up when they were supposed to. Some people cannot receive certain truths from the Word of God. No matter what you say to them, they still cannot see it, no matter how hard you try to convince them.

RECEIVING, MANIFESTING, AND IMPLEMENTING THE WORD OF GOD

> *Your weakness is not an excuse for sin; you must come to a point where you take the grace of God and resolve the issue with His strength.*

If this truth is in the Word of God and is for us today, then you have to receive it. Once you receive it, it will manifest so that you can implement it in your life. When the truth does not manifest, it is not God working against you; someone else is stopping you, or something else is working in the situation. I tell you this because if there is resistance and something contrary to the fruit of the Spirit, you have to label it. You cannot put it off and say, "Oh, that's just

them," or "That's just me." If these characteristics do not match up
with a manifestation of the Spirit, they must be dealt with.

> *Now faith is the substance of things hoped for, the*
> *evidence of things not seen.*
>
> —Hebrews 11:1

Your weakness is not an excuse for sin; you must come to a point
where you take the grace of God and resolve the issue with His
strength. According to Hebrews 11:1, God asks us to have faith,
which is "the substance of things hoped for, and the evidence of
things not seen." This verse talks about resolution. If we are in a
faith deficit, that is our weakness because we need something that
we don't have. We must move toward resolution and cannot accept
anything but what God has already shown us. That is what Hebrews
11:1 means.

Our attitude must be, "Well, then, I must receive this. I am going
from deficit or weakness to strength or provision, a process of
fulfillment." When you order something, it will be delivered to you,
and eventually, you will receive it. I will not worry about things like
losing my salvation or missing out on what God has for me because
I understand those blessings. They are set because I have confessed
Jesus as Lord, am saved, and am walking out my salvation in fear
and trembling (Philippians 2:12).

I pray in the Spirit and am submissive to God, so I will not miss out on what God has for me. I walk in certain strengths now because God has already provided for me. I feel I am going somewhere in other areas, but I am not there yet. However, I do not focus on the weakness of not having what I want. I focus on the fact that I have the substance of things hoped for and the evidence in my hand. I believe that I receive what I have asked for; even though I do not have the manifestation yet. I know it in the Spirit. A transition, a process, is taking place.

If you are frustrated, want to see results in your life, or wish to get rid of certain bad habits, you have to turn your weaknesses over to God and let His fire burn them out. Let the fire of God, the resurrection power of the Holy Spirit, revive you and lift you up so that those strengths manifest. This provision is spiritual and will become physical. You do not want to get addicted to anything or rely on other crutches; you want to run to God, turn yourself in, and move from weakness to strength and provision. That is what Paul was talking about in Romans 8.

Joshua turned himself into God and went from weakness to strength. He was formed into a leader in his deficit as he waited on God and Moses, but Joshua was not recognized as a leader at that time. Afterward, Joshua ended up taking Moses's place. He was perfect for the job because he experienced everything Moses had experienced. Even though Joshua was not recognized at the time, he endured his process. Even though he appeared to be just a servant, Joshua ended up being a leader, which is what will happen with you.

Jesus wants us to identify with Him. He was a strength to many people when He was in this world. However, even though He was everyone's strength, He was hated and killed. Jesus was in the garden of Gethsemane praying and all His disciples fell asleep, and not even one person helped or supported Him in prayer (Matthew 26:36–46). Jesus asked them if they could not even stay awake an hour to pray with Him, but they fell asleep. As He is, so are we in this world (1 John 4:17). Jesus relied on God, the Father, in His weakness. The Bible says that Jesus learned obedience by what He suffered (Hebrews 5:8). We often find ourselves alone and weak, yet the Holy Spirit is with us, so we can find strength in Him.

No matter what we are going through, we must eventually go from weakness to strength. The books written in Heaven about you talk about how God, in your weakness, made you strong, so you will finish strong (Psalm 139:16). You will accomplish so much, but at times, you feel as if you are not going to make it another day. Remember, you are in transition because you are going from your deficit to your provision.

4

FROM GENERATION TO GENERATION

One generation shall praise Your works to another, and
shall declare Your mighty acts.
—Psalm 145:4

We have witnessed many events in this generation and should desire to be part of seeing God's faithfulness displayed. We should be moved to intercede, believe, and be part of what God is doing so that we can hand off what we have learned to the next generation. We should be able to report God's faithfulness to the next generation, which means we must break some curses off the bloodlines. Our responsibility in our generation is to prevent passing on the curses that may be in our bloodlines.

Believers must execute what God has already done; He already destroyed the works of the devil, but this needs to be enforced (1 John 3:8). If we do not do that, we are not fulfilling the purpose of the church of Jesus Christ on the earth. Instead, we are allowing evil spirits to come against that generation successfully. Evil spirits can enforce the curse when it should not even exist. The problems that we have today from the highest level down to the family level should not be happening.

STOPPING CURSES FROM TRANSFERRING TO THE NEXT GENERATION

Issues resulting from curses are not permitted in the lives of God's people, and yet they are happening because we have not been proactive. Most have not been educated to understand this. I will not allow certain matters to operate, which means that I will stop curses from being transferred to the next generation. I do this by educating and informing people. You can do this too. We must equip people to understand that when they address these evil spirits, they will not be allowed to work any longer and will not return.

For example, Joseph was sent to Egypt ahead of his family, even though his brothers tragically sold him into slavery (Genesis 37:18–36). Even though it was not God's will for all that to happen, God still used it and sent Joseph ahead. He interpreted the dreams of Pharaoh, the king of Egypt. There were to be seven years of plenty and seven years of famine. Joseph blessed Egypt, but he was really sent to help his family and the Israelites. As Joseph grew in favor, he eventually brought his father, brothers, and entire family from Israel to Egypt to survive the famine and be preserved (Genesis 47:1–17).

Unfortunately, the next Pharaoh did not remember Joseph (Exodus 1:1–8). So how did it happen that the Israelites then served four hundred years of slavery in Egypt (Genesis 15:13)? If Joseph was sent ahead of time to preserve his family line, genealogies, generations, and bloodline, how did slavery happen? It happened because their freedom was never enforced, and they became enslaved. Moses had to deliver the Israelites from Egypt, and he led them into the desert toward the promised land, and you know all the children of Israel went through the promised land in the desert.

If you remember, Joseph was sent to Egypt, and when his family came, they settled in Canaan, so they were *already in the promised land.*

> *Now the report of it was heard in Pharaoh's house, saying, "Joseph's brothers have come." So it pleased Pharaoh and his servants well. And Pharaoh*

said to Joseph, "Say to your brothers, 'Do this: Load
your animals and depart; go to the land of Canaan.
Bring your father and your households and come to
me; I will give you the best of the land of Egypt, and
you will eat the fat of the land.'"

—Genesis 45:16–18

They only moved down to Goshen in Egypt during the famine, and then they lived there for four hundred years before being led back to Canaan. It is written in history that God used Moses to deliver His people, but think about it: Joseph's family came out of Canaan hundreds of years earlier (Genesis 37:1–25). They were already in the promised land.

Generations and bloodlines are significant, but if we are not proactive, we will see sin patterns crop up again, repeating themselves. You can see this happening throughout the Bible and repeating in history, even in our nation, America. I see repeats of battles we have already won. Then we have to fight again for what we already fought for. Our privileges are taken away because we were not diligent in holding on to them. This happens when we are not mindful, but that is not how it should be.

God has a way of dealing with us and our bloodlines. You are not only dealing with these issues for yourself. You should tell yourself that *this will not be transferred to my children and will not go to the next generation.* You stop certain curses by finding how life should be in the Word and then enforcing that. Then you can go even further. You say to yourself, *I will now teach other families and my church, minister to people wherever God sends me, and stop this curse from working in their lives.* So you teach other people to take a stand so that history does not have to repeat itself. In other words, you should not have to fight for things twice.

JESUS MADE A SHOW OF THE DEVIL OPENLY

We have been talking about how Jesus made a show of the devil openly, defeated him, and went around doing good and healing everyone oppressed by the devil (Colossians 2:15; Acts 10:38). Yet believers sit around and argue about if healing is for today, if God wants us to be poor or rich, if He wants us to give or not give, if we should tithe or not, and other controversial matters. They argue about whether or not devils can even bother a Christian. We end up revisiting matters that were not questioned at the turn of the century or even when the church was formed. But now, these topics are questioned. We go through these cycles because we are not diligent in reinforcing what has already been given.

> *We should be passing on a legacy to the next generation in our family line and the body of Christ on the earth.*

The bloodlines represent generations of families who have been given a heritage, an inheritance, passed from one generation to another. We should be passing on a legacy to the next generation in our family line and the body of Christ on the earth. We should be handing it over and giving them a greater legacy than we have encountered; we should be handing off a greater inheritance.

Jesus walked in the power of the Holy Spirit. He was crucified and went to the belly of the earth for three days, then He was raised from the dead. After His resurrection, He walked around for forty days in power (Acts 1:3; 1 Corinthians 15:4–6). However, the Holy Spirit Himself was the power that rose Jesus from the dead. So many times, we end up fighting battles for issues that should already be settled. The apostle Paul showed us that everything obtained through the finished work of the cross and the resurrection of Jesus is done; we do not need to revisit it or do it over again. As the saying goes, we should not reinvent the wheel. Certain truths in the Bible are indisputable, yet we sit around and argue about these matters.

THE SAME POWER THAT ROSE JESUS FROM THE DEAD LIVES IN YOU

But if the Spirit of Him who raised Jesus from the dead dwells in you, He who raised Christ from the dead will also give life to your mortal bodies through His Spirit Who dwells in you.

—Romans 8:11

The same power that rose Jesus from the dead now dwells in you. The Holy Spirit can quicken your mortal body, which means you could be healed and unable to explain it. You could suddenly have an answer when you didn't have that answer before. Suddenly, the Lord could show you, answer you, or deliver you, even though you did not know what was happening. Suddenly, an evil spirit that was bothering you could leave. You wouldn't know why or how; you would only know it was gone.

The Holy Spirit is on a much higher level than we are and has done more in the past than we even realize. God trusts us by putting His Spirit within us. The Holy Spirit is beyond our comprehension, yet He lives in us. Unfortunately, we do not seem to encounter Him in His fullness, but that is not His fault. That is our fault because we have not correctly handed the inheritance off to the next generation.

We need to have the pure teachings of Jesus and the disciples, and we should have the same experiences they had. We should be experiencing what happened on the day of Pentecost. We should have the manifestation of the Spirit that Paul talked about in Corinthians. This should be happening for us personally and in all our gatherings. It does not happen because we do not understand generations and family bloodlines. Most do not understand spiritual warfare regarding the bloodlines and what we are dealing with today.

WE HAVE BEEN GIVEN ALL THINGS THAT PERTAIN TO LIFE AND GODLINESS

As His divine power has given to us all things that pertain to life and godliness, through the knowledge of Him Who called us by glory and virtue, by which have been given to us exceedingly great and precious promises, that through these you may be partakers of the divine nature, having escaped the corruption that is in the world through lust.

—2 Peter 1:3–4

Everything we need for life and godliness has already been given to us through the power that dwells in us. We can see that God is a better Father than we know and has already provided all these things for us. They are already deposited within us. We have whatever we need to live out this life in full power and provision; we should partake of the divine nature and manifest it. Peter tells us that it has already been deposited in us through the divine power of the Holy Spirit. You should read this verse every day because it will put an end to the curses that transfer from one generation to the other.

> *Or what man is there among you who, if his son asks*
> *for bread, will give him a stone? Or if he asks for a*
> *fish, will he give him a serpent? If you then, being*
> *evil, know how to give good gifts to your children,*
> *how much more will your Father Who is in Heaven*
> *give good things to those who ask Him!*
>
> —Matthew 7:9–11

As Jesus said, our earthly fathers would not give us a stone if we asked for bread or a serpent if we asked for a fish, so how much more will our Heavenly Father give us when we ask Him? I do not doubt that our Father in Heaven desires to give us the kingdom. God is a good God Who is handing us what we need. I understand that I am under the blessing because God blesses His children. If God has a plan and it is His good pleasure to give us His kingdom, I will believe that my bloodline and my generation will prosper (Luke 12:32).

CURSE BREAKERS ENFORCE THE COVENANT

From now on, these evil spirits will no longer be able to operate in my bloodline. When I go to conferences, twelve hundred people may be there, with potentially almost that many family lines and bloodlines represented. If I release the Word of life there and break curses, those curses will not be passed on to the next generation. If you minister to people and tell them what we are talking about here, you can stop these curses from transferring to future bloodlines in other families and genealogies, which is what I want you to do. I want you to minister to people and stop this from continuing to happen.

Suddenly, when bloodline curses are broken, we will see people who walk on water, don't sink, and no longer doubt. We will see people who succeed in their generations, and their children will grow up to be miracle workers, gospel preachers, prophets, apostles, pastors, teachers, and evangelists. They will tell others of God's goodness, preaching to their generation and breaking curses. These curse breakers will enforce the covenant, talk about the goodness of God, and see people repent. An overthrow of the enemy and wrong mindsets will happen so that the next generation will not encounter those setbacks. People are already sprinkled throughout the world who are uprooting strongholds and putting demonic forces under their feet. This could happen so much more in this generation.

The uprooting of strongholds and spiritual revolution could happen in our generation; I believe this for all our Warrior Notes students. At this writing, we have between eighteen and nineteen thousand students. Can you imagine if every one of them continued to disperse the good news and cut off all these evil spirits from working in their bloodlines? If each of you spread this information to thousands of people in your lifetime, you would be affecting millions. We could see this turn in our generation by discerning what is said here and ending these demonic influences in our bloodlines.

> *Be encouraged that you are important in the day you live in; you have a message of deliverance and good news that people need to hear.*

And He has made from one blood every nation of men to dwell on all the face of the earth, and has determined their preappointed times and the boundaries of their dwellings.

—Acts 17:26

The Lord has predetermined the times and seasons when people will be born, He has set their boundaries, and all truth has already been established. God has already done this as spoken in the book of Acts. Jesus told the disciples, "It is not for you to know times or seasons which the Father has put in His own authority" (Acts 1:7). God's times and seasons are not for us to know or understand; only the Father knows and predetermines them. God has established His plan for the nations and people living on the earth. Be encouraged that you are important in the day you live in; you have a message of deliverance and good news that people need to hear.

I deal with people's real problems by dealing with the root. I will tell them that bloodlines have been assigned familiar spirits, which are there to enforce a curse in a territory with family lines, and that we can break that. We can stop that from ever happening again. We can see that curse reversed, which is what I want you to do. I want you to be the true answer to people that want to know the truth. If people don't desire to know the truth, you don't have to talk to them.

Multitudes of people who wanted help followed Jesus around. Why? Because they were poor, sick, and demonized. Jesus said the gospel message was good news to heal the sick and bring deliverance from the devil. He proclaimed the year of Jubilee and debt cancellation; He broke yokes and raised people from the dead. The people who needed freedom followed Jesus because He had the answer. We are called to minister to people this same way; we have the answer and must tell people about it.

The demons will be terrified of you and will not want you to speak. They will not want you to show up because they know they will lose people. The demons cannot influence the people anymore because when they know the truth, the truth will set them free (John 8:31–32). God wants to sever the influence those demons have on you and your family, and then He wants to use you to sever and stop that influence in other people's lives.

God will prove you by bringing you into situations that cause you to grow. He will see how you respond to these situations and then mature you. As you gain knowledge, you will become trustworthy, and then you will be put into leadership. Once you overcome your domain and overthrow all the evil spirits assigned to your bloodline, God will send you to other people. Then you will see the overthrow in their lives. It is a step-by-step process, and God trusts you.

Remember that you are on an accelerated course in learning, and the whole goal is that you overcome because He overcame for you, and then you teach other people how to overcome.

Wherever you go and whatever you do, be mindful that these evil spirits do not want to let go of the people you encounter whether unsaved or saved. The demons influence people based on how much they hand themselves to them. Christians can allow evil spirits to control them if their wills have been given over to those evil spirits. They might have allowed evil spirits to influence their minds, wills, emotions, and bodies, but not in their spirits.

At the same time, satan used Peter because he had wrong thoughts, and he spoke them (Matthew 16:22–23). You must be faithful to let God train you as you put yourself in the position for the holy fire to burn out the chaff and teach you. You will then encounter deliverance, overthrow, and cleansing by the Holy Spirit and fire. As you grow spiritually and go into overthrow, you will then be able to minister this to others.

Why did Jesus have to go through what He went through? It says that "though He was a son, yet He learned obedience by the things which He suffered" (Hebrews 5:8). Even growing up, Jesus grew in the training and admonition of the Lord (Luke 2:40–51; Ephesians 6:4). Once He reached a certain age, He was launched into ministry.

Jesus, the Son of God, had to go through situations as a human being, just as we do. However, Jesus was known as the Son of Man because He submitted as a servant and did not consider equality with God as something to cling to (Philippians 2:5–11). We have to look at what Jesus did and what He went through. He was tempted in the desert and passed all His tests, just like you will pass all your tests.

You are the solution for your generation, family, and bloodline, but you are also the solution for the generations to come. We have the gospel message, deliverance, faith, and healing on our lips. We have that message on our lips and anointing in our hands.

HOLY FIRE: THE KINGDOM OF GOD

5

WILLING AND OBEDIENT

If you are willing and obedient, You shall eat
The good of the land.
—Isaiah 1:19

The move of God has to manifest itself through willing people. God's angels are here, and we see this mighty move starting in the Spirit. Yet many manifestations in the flesh and the soul realm have hindered us. God has already planned for everything related to our genealogies and bloodlines. He gave us a resolution ahead of time. Yet evil spirits have plans to propagate their agenda and enforce curses, so you see characteristics transferred to the next generation.

It is no coincidence that people in the next generation struggle with the same sins the previous generation did. By tracing their sins, you can see that an evil spirit has been assigned to that bloodline, enforcing the curse, which needs to be overthrown. The problem is that people need to know the truth, but hearing it does not necessarily cause it to manifest. You can listen to the truth, but then you must receive it in your heart and understand it. How often have you been told something and then you forget it, or somebody tells you something, and you turn around and cannot repeat or do what they said?

HEARTFELT FAITH

For assuredly, I say to you, whoever says to this mountain, "Be removed and be cast into the sea," and does not doubt in his heart, but believes that those things he says will be done, he will have whatever he says.

—Mark 11:23

You must absorb the truth; Jesus explained that we must comprehend and understand it. It is heartfelt faith. You speak to your mountains from your heart; believe it and speak with your mouth. It is not mental agreement, which is limited to your thoughts. What Jesus tells you has to be received in your heart and become part of you. It is like bread from Heaven. You partake of Jesus by eating the Word of God. You take Him into you; He changes you by becoming a part of you.

The Word of God changes you. Then from that place of change, in that soil of your heart, you speak and produce a crop. You can move mountains with your words. In this generation, we have to be careful not to just mentally agree because we will not see the power of our faith. It has to be transferred into your heart and become part of your heart and spiritual being. Jesus explained that many people just mentally agree; however, it is not only what you hear because you can hear and not understand. So faith is about what you understand.

The disciples asked Jesus, "Why do You speak to them in parables?" He answered and said to them, 'Because it has been given to you to know the mysteries of the kingdom of heaven, but to them it has not been given'" (Matthew 13:10–11). Jesus would explain the deep mysteries of the kingdom to His disciples, but He would not mention them in a public setting, which is a mystery. If God has chosen you to understand things, it takes you far beyond those who only hear it.

YOU MUST TAKE WHAT YOU HEAR, THEN UNDERSTAND AND APPLY IT

Out of a whole class of students, only two will excel and reach the goal out of a large group of people. They are assigned the prize positions. They excel not by reciting the information but by comprehending and performing it. It is a matter of whether they can achieve it. In other words, can they apply what they heard and studied? That gets them promoted, and I have seen this many times.

> *Wisdom is the principal thing; therefore get wisdom.*
> *And in all your getting, get understanding.*
> —Proverbs 4:7

> *Happy (blessed, fortunate, enviable) is the man who*
> *finds skillful and godly Wisdom, and the man who*
> *gets understanding [drawing it forth from God's*
> *Word and life's experiences].*
> —Proverbs 3:13 AMPC

You can have a group of people who all want to be successful. They all study and sacrifice, but they fail when it comes to getting into that situation and performing. The people that are chosen for that job or position can perform what they have learned. It is the same with the gospel and what we deal with in this generation. Jesus told me that it is not just what you hear but what you understand. In everything you do, pursue wisdom and gain understanding. I can have the knowledge and spout it off, but do I understand what I just said? You may have a word of knowledge but cannot apply it if you don't have a word of wisdom.

> *In this generation, we are supposed to gain wisdom through experience. This is called experiential knowledge.*

At times, Jesus asked me if I understood what He was saying, and if I didn't, I let Him explain it to me. I have had to say things that God intends to happen, and even though I do not understand them, He tells me to say certain words. Other times, He gives me an understanding of it. The enemy does not understand everything. In this generation, we are supposed to gain wisdom through experience. This is called experiential knowledge. I can ask the Lord to unveil the truth, and He can do that, but I might not understand what I see or even know what it is. At that point, does it really help me?

However, if the Lord explains why something is happening, what is needed, and how to apply it, I gain a deeper understanding. Then you can teach people the dynamics of what the Lord is saying. It is not just hearing the Word of God—it is also understanding. Even though "faith comes by hearing and hearing by the word of God," you must reach the place where you have the wisdom to know how to apply it (Romans 10:17).

Jesus wants to take us further than we thought we could go, but it will take understanding. It will take seeing why we are the way we are and why things happen. I am not going to accept the fact that God has mysteries, and we might not ever know what just happened there. God wants to explain mysteries concerning the supernatural to us so that we can hear and understand them if we have ears to hear. I can get healed and not understand healing, but I am not talking about things like that. You do not even have to study healing to get healed. You could believe that the Lord will heal you, and He could heal you. He could touch you now, and you could be completely healed and not even understand what happened.

However, I am speaking of dealing with our generation and everything that happens within that generation. We are dealing with people's behaviors and personalities and their decisions for and against us. We must not deal with opinions but with established truths in Heaven, even when the truth is presented as opinions. Certain instructions from the Lord are presented to us as though we have a choice, but we do not, so this requires us to have a higher level of discernment. In this generation, God wants us to understand the warfare around us, which concerns the demonic enforcing curses.

Jesus wants us to understand how He operated. When we study Matthew 8:23–34, and Luke 8:22–39, we see that Jesus wanted to go to the other side of the lake with his disciples. While on the boat, they encountered a great storm, and Jesus was asleep. For fear of perishing, the disciples finally had to wake Him up. Jesus rebuked the wind, and they safely reached the other side. After arrival, Jesus dealt with a demoniac by casting the devil out, and then He got back in the boat and returned. Still, that only took several hours, and Jesus hardly had time to get out of the boat. We must understand why that storm came up because this story has a deeper meaning.

The Father told Jesus to go to the other side. So Jesus said, "Let us cross over to the other side of the lake," and they launched out, which meant they were going to make it (Luke 8:22). All the training that Jesus gave His disciples was so that every one of them could do the works that He did. He was training them to take over the ministry one day and do even greater works (John 14:12).

Jesus fell asleep because the Father had told them they were going to the other side. It did not matter what happened; Jesus did not doubt it. Instead of waking Jesus up, the disciples should have taken authority and spoken to the winds and the waves, commanding them to cease and be still, but they did not. It was the same in other matters: The disciples did not take authority when they should have.

Another time, they could not cast devils out when they were told they had authority over them (Matthew 17:14–19). We miss some of these insights, and we don't have the needed understanding and wisdom. When we get to the other side of the lake, we see a territorial demon with two thousand demons inside a demon-possessed man (Mark 5:1–20). Jesus confronted him, cast the demons out, and then got right back in the boat to go back and didn't even stay. The whole reason they went over to the other side was to take out that demon.

However, the disciples should have stopped the storm. That territorial spirit caused the storm in an attempt to take them all out before they even got there. We don't discern this was all warfare. Most who read this account do not notice that Jesus did not even stay for lunch; He didn't do anything except cast out those demons, then He got right back in the boat and went back to the other side. That was all Jesus was sent to do: deliver the area of the territorial unclean spirit.

The Holy Spirit wants us to glean from that experience and understand warfare. Through this passage of Scripture, we are taught to recognize the curse that was going on in that region. We must observe how Jesus destroyed the powers of the enemy.

Jesus was doing warfare, which we must discern. All the accounts of Jesus's life and ministry in the Bible and everything that Paul and the apostles taught are given to us for our generation. Even though a previous generation read the same verses, we need to have a revelation of them in this generation. We must understand what the Holy Spirit is saying in order to wage war properly. In this generation, we do not have to put up with what the previous generation had to because the Holy Spirit is working with us, giving us greater revelation. When Jesus returned to the boat, He had accomplished what He was supposed to do.

CENTURION FAITH

None of the disciples and the people that Jesus dealt with were commended for their faith like the Roman centurion was, and he was not even Jewish. Jesus was not sent to the Romans but to the Jews. Jesus selected twelve disciples, and the Roman centurion was not chosen as a disciple. Yet Jesus marveled and said, "I have not found such great faith, not even in Israel!" (Matthew 8:10). The

Roman centurion was not part of the covenant and had not followed Jesus. He had not heard Jesus's teachings and was not a chosen one, yet he got it. The centurion was commended for his faith and is mentioned in the Bible forever.

What did the centurion understand that the disciples missed, even though they were with Jesus for three-and-a-half years? I want to show you that you do not have to have all the things that you think you need to get it. God has given you the Holy Spirit, the Word of God, and you have the availability to excel. You do not have to have lived with Jesus for three-and-a-half years to do the works of Jesus.

> *The centurion answered and said, "Lord, I am not worthy that You should come under my roof. But only speak a word, and my servant will be healed. For I also am a man under authority, having soldiers under me. And I say to this one, 'Go,' and he goes; and to another, 'Come,' and he comes; and to my servant, 'Do this,' and he does it."*
>
> *—Matthew 8:8–9*

That centurion got it because he understood authority. He understood and discerned that Jesus was the Messiah. The centurion explained that his servants under him obey his commands, so he knew that if Jesus gave the word, it would be done. Jesus never even came to his house, but he got it!

In this generation, we will have centurion faith. In our school, conferences, and partners, I am instilling centurion faith in us to understand authority so that we reach a place where we can hear from God. We must say, "Lord, I know what Your will is. Just speak the word, and it will be done." Then we must refuse to accept anything else.

The Lord can command your bloodline, family, and generation right now. You commit to the Lord and say, "Lord, only speak a word, and it will be done," then wait on Him. Once the Lord speaks that word, you change your generation, family, and yourself because you now have God's word on it. When God speaks, He speaks a blessing over your family, and the devil's plans will not prevail. Evil will stop because you put a stop to it.

> *Do not wait for this to go to another generation; you need to put a stop to the enemy's plan right now.*

GOD WILL SHOW HIMSELF STRONG FOR THOSE WHOSE HEARTS ARE LOYAL TO HIM

I was sent back to tell people, "Listen, you need to be the one. Do not wait for someone else to do it." Do not wait for this to go to another generation; *you* need to put a stop to the enemy's plan right now. You can change and reroute history. You can change everything, and you do that through having centurion faith. You must understand authority and refuse to take no for an answer. You must understand God's will and not accept anything else; refuse to bend. I will see extraordinary things happen in this generation because I refuse to accept anything except what God wants.

The devil fears a person who is convinced of God's will. You are called to be an ambassador of Heaven (2 Corinthians 5:20). When you have faith like the centurion and understand authority, you become one who supports God's covenant in this generation. God can use a person like that.

I encourage you to have heartfelt faith; believe and say, "Lord, just speak. Tell me, and I will believe and do it." No matter what it looks like, this generation does not have to see the end concerning the antichrist and the evil that seems to surround us. This has happened many times before. We can stand against the enemy's plan and reap a massive harvest of souls. We do not have to allow this evil. It cycles through, and we can prevent it. We can stop it and see a harvest of souls come in.

> *For the eyes of the LORD run to and fro throughout the whole earth, to show Himself strong on behalf of those whose heart is loyal to Him. In this you have done foolishly; therefore from now on you shall have wars.*
>
> —2 Chronicles 16:9

In 2 Chronicles 16:9, the people did not discern the Lord, and God said they were foolish. Yet the eyes of the Lord are going back and forth today, looking for someone whose heart is loyal to Him—that is us in this generation. So we must raise our hands and say, "Lord, use me. I am loyal to You, and I will stop this. I will see Your heart's desire come to pass in this generation." Once this has happened to you and your family, you can help others by overthrowing evil. This is what I want to see. I encourage you to have centurion faith and say, "Lord, I agree with whatever is written about me in Heaven. Speak it over me, over my family, and over my generation."

Even if the majority are like the unbelieving children of Israel who did not enter the promised land, at least you can be like Joshua and

Caleb, like them, you can say, "We are well able to do this" (Numbers 13:30). Remember that if you are willing and obedient, you will eat the good of the land (Isaiah 1:19). Even if it is only us, just a small remnant, God will favor us. You do not have to be drawn in by the unbelief and doubt of a generation. You can eat of the good of the land. Let God use us in our generation and break those curses. Let us see this thing turned around for good. May God use us to change history.

6

REVELATION TO VISITATION

*And God said, "Let us make man in our
image, after our likeness…"*
—Genesis 1:26

The Lord wants everyone to have the revelation of Who He is.
Once we realize who He is, we also realize who we are
because we were created in His image. In the beginning, God made
us in His image, which is important to understand. The church and
those coming into the kingdom must know how much God cares for
and values people. God is looking for people who are dedicated to
Him and whose heart is loyal to Him; God will strengthen and help
them. However, in 2 Chronicles 16:9, the children of Israel had
chosen to do foolishly, so they encountered war.

Once we know Who God is, our value is known in Heaven; we realize He is loyal to us because we are loyal to Him. There is an exchange between God and man, which is when you become a friend of God. This occurs when you have fully allowed the holy fire and sanctification process, the purging and the purifying process, to manifest in your life. As you begin to mature, God will trust you more. In these last days, a remnant is giving themselves fully over to God.

THE REMNANT CHOOSES THE NARROW WAY

Enter by the narrow gate; for wide is the gate and broad is the way that leads to destruction, and there are many who go in by it. Because narrow is the gate and difficult is the way which leads to life, and there are few who find it.

—Matthew 7:13–14

This remnant is a group of people choosing the narrow way; they are people in churches all over the world. Many people are in churches and religious organizations that have grown cold. Today, many situations mirror what happened in the first several chapters of the book of Revelation with the seven churches. As a result, some believers are hungry for more of God. They want to be loyal to God and have a relationship with Him; they want more than what they experience at their organization. They are willing to meet with people in small groups for prayer, Bible study, and fellowship.

Since the world system is corrupt, the remnant desires to take care of each other. They also advocate for homeschooling, which is what we are doing at Warrior Notes. We are going with the flow of what is happening as people migrate out of the established churches and want to form Bible study groups and get educated outside the world system. Homeschooling is government-approved, but it is Bible-based. Different denominations were formed in moves of God throughout history, which developed into organizations. But these grew cold as they got bigger.

In past cycles, we have needed revival or a movement to take people out of ungodly situations in schools. These cycles keep going on and on, which you can see throughout history. God's will is not for us to grow cold or become so big that we don't meet people's needs and cannot function anymore. The kingdom of God on earth should keep growing and growing until Jesus comes back, but that is not how it works down here in this fallen world.

The fivefold ministry of the church seems to have gotten away from talking about our heavenly value. Most are not discussing Who God is or the holy fire and holiness. In my book *The Mystery of the Power*

Words, I explain why certain subjects are not spoken about anymore. When you see this happening, you can see why believers must migrate and find the right track where the full gospel is being preached again. God is searching throughout the whole earth to build up the remnant and strengthen those whose hearts are loyal to Him.

JESUS, THE NAME ABOVE ALL NAMES

Therefore God also has highly exalted Him and given Him the name which is above every name, that at the name of Jesus every knee should bow, of those in Heaven, and of those on earth, and of those under the earth, and that every tongue should confess that Jesus Christ is Lord, to the glory of God the Father.

—Philippians 2:9–11

When God moves, we need to stay with the pure message of the gospel and enforce what He is really saying. I often listen to sermons from different people and organizations and check the temperature with them to see what's popular. I see what most people watch and then look at the offered content. I have been shocked that hundreds of thousands of people are watching certain people that never mention the name of Jesus. Jesus's name is never in any of their titles, comments, or quotes. The word "God" is used but not "Jesus."

The demons are afraid of the name of Jesus because His name invokes full authority, and He has the name above all names.

> *The name of Jesus is so powerful that it paralyzes the demonic and sets people free at the mention of it.*

Did you know that when you go on a secular TV show, you are not allowed to mention the name of Jesus? (I can name the shows.) You can mention the name of God, but you cannot say the name of Jesus. I wondered about that because individuals would tell me they were on this or that show and were not allowed to say Jesus's name. If they did say it, it was bleeped out. When I attended different secular productions, I was told that also, and I realized what it was. The name of Jesus is so powerful that it paralyzes the demonic and sets people free at the mention of it. I was thinking, *Why would people fear the name of Jesus on secular TV?* Then I realized those demons don't want Jesus's name over the airwaves.

When I listened to different ministers and noticed they were not using the name of Jesus at all, I realized that the prince of the power of the air was starting to infiltrate and influence those ministers. I do not know if they were aware or did it on purpose. In my book

The Mystery of the Power Words, the Lord gave me those words; some are actually phrases and subjects. It is called *The Mystery of the Power Words* because satan does not want us to use certain very powerful words, subjects, and phrases anymore. If you take that list and listen to Christian ministers, you can check off every time these words are mentioned. Sometimes, none of these words will be mentioned in an hour-long sermon.

THE HOLY SPIRIT GIVES YOU THE BOLDNESS TO PROPHESY AND WITNESS

I first realized this probably twenty years ago, so I started to keep track, noticing how certain words and subjects were missing from the teachings. Recently, I checked again, and it is still happening. Throughout cycles of church history, the system would become ineffective and no longer meet the needs of the people. People who are hungry and seeking God migrate out; if you talk to them, they are looking for the fire of God. They are looking for a move of God and the Word of God that is preached with fire. They are looking for a hot meal, spiritually speaking, and want to encounter the presence and power of God. They want to encounter the Holy Spirit, Who gives them boldness at work to prophesy and witness.

> *I know your works, that you are neither cold nor hot.*
> *I could wish you were cold or hot. So then, because*

*you are lukewarm, and neither cold nor hot, I will
vomit you out of My mouth.*

—Revelation 3:15–16

I have often studied history, and I have seen these trends before. I know how the church goes through cycles, which is very predictable. In some cycles, the temperature changes overall, which is consistent with the content that is preached. If certain truths, words, and concepts from the Word of God are removed, the message isn't as hot, so the people aren't as hot. Their spiritual diet is not producing the characteristics of a hot church that Jesus wanted. In the book of Revelation, Jesus wanted them to decide if they were hot or cold, but He never wanted them to be lukewarm. Of course, Jesus wanted them to be hot but encouraged them to decide.

In 1 and 2 Corinthians, Paul wrote to the church of Corinth, and you realize that much of what is going on today was happening to the Corinthians at that time. Paul addressed carnality and people who thought they were spiritual because they were being used in the gifts, yet the flesh ruled them. When you read Romans 7 and 8, then Corinthians, you can see the contrast between how Paul addressed the people in Rome and those in Corinth.

And I, brethren, could not speak to you as to spiritual people but as to carnal, as to babes in Christ. I fed you with milk and not with solid food; for until now you were not able to receive it, and even now you are still not able; for you are still carnal. For where there are envy, strife, and divisions among you, are you not carnal and behaving like mere men?

—1 Corinthians 3:1–3

Paul wanted the Corinthians to stop drinking baby milk, grow out of diapers, and get on the meat of the word. It was time for them to change their diet and mature into adults. Paul wanted to address the Corinthians as mature adults but said he could not because they were carnal. Paul wanted to take them on to deeper things, but he couldn't because the Corinthians were immature.

That happened at a Bible college I attended. The president of the college, who was also a teacher, said the Lord would not let him go on to teach the deeper things that he knew. The Lord had shown him so much, but he was not allowed to teach it yet. The Lord told him that the people had not gotten the basics of what they were already taught. They had just not received it, and he was constantly repeating himself and going over the same teachings again and again. The president had to explain to those frustrated with the repetitive teaching that he was doing it on purpose because the Lord told him they hadn't gotten it yet. He told us that we would hear the same teaching every year until we went on with the Lord. It really shocked me because I knew he was right.

I was a younger student at the time, and I thought, *I'm ready*. We always think we are ready for something until it happens. Then we realize we are not prepared, and reality sets in. However, this is where God has you today. He was looking throughout the earth, and He found you, and He highly esteems and values you because you highly esteem and value Him, and you want to go on with Him. You might not be able to find a church or gathering that meets up to the standard or the fire you have been exposed to already through Warrior Notes or another organization.

You may be looking for groups of people who have a passion for seeking God, want the narrow way, want to walk in holiness, and be on fire for God, which is why we formed Warrior Notes Fellowships and Warrior Notes Churches. We already have different apps, such as Warrior Notes TV and the Warrior Notes Chat, and we will soon have Warrior Notes Health. We are planning many different programs for children and parents because we want groups of people with a passion for God to get together.

If the eyes of the Lord are running throughout the earth and He has found you, then He will provide a way for you to fellowship with people of like passion, which is what Warrior Notes is all about. We are connecting people worldwide, and then we will form an army ready to evangelize. We will teach, preach, and get people on the same page with God to see this end-time harvest come in.

REVELATION, VISITATION, AND HABITATION: THE STAGES OF YOUR RELATIONSHIP WITH GOD

[For I always pray to] the God of our Lord Jesus Christ, the Father of glory, that He may grant you a spirit of wisdom and revelation [of insight into mysteries and secrets] in the [deep and intimate] knowledge of Him, By having the eyes of your heart flooded with light, so that you can know and understand the hope to which He has called you, and how rich is His glorious inheritance in the saints (His set-apart ones), And [so that you can know and understand] what is the immeasurable and unlimited and surpassing greatness of His power in and for us who believe, as demonstrated in the working of His mighty strength. Which He exerted in Christ when

He raised Him from the dead and seated Him at His
[own] right hand in the heavenly [places].
—Ephesians 1:17–20 AMPC

When God favors you, knows who you are, and sees that you highly esteem Him, He will want to help you. He does that by getting closer to you in proximity. There are stages of your relationship with God. First, the Holy Spirit comes and gives you revelation of the Word of God. So the first stage you can expect is revelation. In other words, the Holy Spirit, according to Ephesians 1:17–19, will come in, and He will open the eyes of your heart. The Holy Spirit will actually flood you with light, which will expose the truth so that it rises to the surface.

As soon as you see that, you will be astounded, and as Paul says, you will know the hope to which you have been called because of the transformative power of truth. Suddenly, you will realize the truth about God and what He is doing for you. You will see that God gives you hope because you have been called to do specific tasks and given certain gifts.

Next, Paul prays that we would know the glorious inheritance in the saints. A table with a delicious meal has been set for us as God's holy people. We can partake of all these wonderful promises and benefits, the divine nature and fellowship with God, and the revelation that comes to us. With this revelation, you understand that the power that rose Jesus from the dead dwells within you. The power of the Holy Spirit is not only dynamite power but also authoritative power.

There are two Greek words, *exousia,* which is the power of authority, and an explosive *dunamis* power, and both are translated in the Bible as power.[1] For example, a law enforcement official has power, which is authority, whereas a soldier is strong and trained for war with brute force. There is the power of authority, and then there is explosive power, and the Holy Spirit gives these to us and reveals the truth about them.

We go through a revelation phase, which is part of our initiation. So phase one is receiving revelation from the Holy Spirit.

As we continue to pray and are exposed to the light, glory, and holy fire, that transformation causes us to be even more curious and want more. At that point, we may start to have visitations and sense the movement of the Holy Spirit, angels, and all kinds of supernatural events around us. Revelation floods our spirits, but we can also have visitations of the Lord's appearance. Some have seen angels or had

---

[1] "Lexicon :: Strong's G1849 – *exousia*," Blue Letter Bible, accessed May 23, 2023, https://www.blueletterbible.org/lexicon/g1849/kjv/tr/0-1/; "Lexicon :: Strong's G1411 – *dynamis*," Blue Letter Bible, accessed May 23, 2023, https://www.blueletterbible.org/lexicon/g1411/kjv/tr/0-1/.

supernatural events happening around them, and they can sense and feel the war between the demonic and the angels. Visitation is when God decides that He is going to come and start to interact with you.

We will have various experiences when God visits us. You can lift your hands even now and start worshiping God, and you will have a visitation because the Holy Spirit will come upon you and wrap you up to help you worship. When you pray, the Holy Spirit will well up within you and help you pray. This process is all part of phase two, visitation. Visitation is when the Lord comes upon you and comes up within you, flowing from the river of life inside you. However, for visitation to happen, you must first be flooded with light, which is phase one, revelation (Ephesians 1:17–23).

The Lord starts this process with you. Once you have revelation, you need to go immediately and sit and worship God, and He will visit you. While you are worshiping Him, quoting the Word of God, speaking to your mountains, praying, and interceding, suddenly, the fire will burn up these barriers inside you. You go to another level where you can handle interaction with the Holy Spirit, angels, and Jesus, and suddenly, another world opens up to you. These interactions should be common occurrences. Every time I raise my hands to worship God, pray, meditate, or study, I expect visitation. Visitation is a constant thing, but it is phase two.

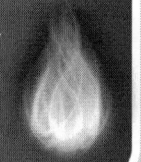

Habitation comes when you have entered God's rest, you have entered the promised land, and the holy fire has had its way with you.

When the Lord notices you because you are seeking Him and want to be loyal to Him, He will separate you, and the fire will come. Then revelation and visitation will come, and the third step is habitation. You will reach a place where the Holy Father has had His way, the fire has had its way, and the Lord has gotten you to a place where you are trustworthy. I never thought I could handle what I can handle now, and I never thought I could do what I am doing now. The boundaries I had set for my life were low, but they seemed very high when I set them, and I have already exceeded those.

Habitation comes when you have entered God's rest, you have entered the promised land, and the holy fire has had its way with you. Then all the barriers, all these things that have hindered you because of traumatic events, are removed. The barriers of hurt, such as being a victim and having a victim spirit or being an orphan with an orphan spirit, are removed. The barriers of feeling abandoned and hurt, always suffering, leave. When the fire of God wins out, displacing these barriers, you go from revelation and visitation to habitation.

7

HABITATION

And My Father will love you so deeply that We will come to
you and make you Our dwelling place.
—John 14:23 TPT

Habitation is when the holy fire has its way and exposes what needs to be removed, starting to burn out all the chaff in us. Once those areas are exposed, they can be destroyed. We are very complicated, intricate, and delicate beings. During this process, you must be patient with the Lord and yourself. If you are going through many hurts and related struggles in your heart and mind, you must understand that you were never made to function in a broken world. You were created to operate at a higher level.

We are dealing with discrepancies, disappointments, and discouragements that should not even exist. We are dealing with problems down here that God never designed us to deal with, and the bottom line is that we go through stress. You must let the Holy Spirit have His way with you to get you to habitation as soon as possible. However, remember it is a process; you cannot hurry it. The healing oil of the Holy Spirit must be applied because hurts must be dealt with and exposed, and deliverance must occur.

HABITATION IS ENTERING THE REST

So when that day comes, you will know that I am living in the Father and that you are one with Me, for I will be living in you. Those who truly love Me are those who obey My commands. Whoever passionately loves Me will be passionately loved by My Father. And I will passionately love you in return and will manifest My life within you . . . Jesus replied, "Loving Me empowers you to obey My word. And My Father will love you so deeply that We will come to you and make you Our dwelling place." ✓

—John 14:20–21, 23 TPT

You may be dealing with real feelings, thoughts, and perceptions, but they are not the truth. The truth is that God highly values you. He has noticed you, you are favored, and He comes in to live with you. As Jesus explained, if you love God, are obedient, and passionately seek Him, He and the Father will come and live with you. That is why I use the word "habitation." As the remnant and the church, we will be purified through the fire, and then we will enter into rest: That is habitation. It is like when Joshua finally took the people to the promised land, and they entered after a trip that should have taken eleven days but instead lasted forty years. (See Deuteronomy 1:2 AMP.)

When you enter that rest and are confident in your habitation, God dwells with you, and you are not afraid that He will leave you. You do not think about losing your salvation or about being abandoned. You do not think of yourself as a victim. You do not doubt that God will answer your prayers; you *know* He will answer. You do not even question if He will listen to you; you know He will hear you. You have entered a place with God that did not seem possible in the past, but you are there. Now, you have to yield to this process. So let the holy fire burn, set yourself apart, and then encounter these three phases: revelation, visitation, and habitation.

YOU ARE BEING PREPARED TO BE A SENT ONE

When the Lord notices you and you start to feel Him drawing you, you will feel as if a change is coming. You are being prepared so that God can send you somewhere; no matter what, you will be effective. Even if people do not respond and you do not see changes, you need to understand that you are on assignment; you must stay on course when you are sent. God is your source, you are giving out, and God takes care of you. You do not need to depend on people's responses; you are sent to them because you are on assignment, so it's a different approach. God is supporting you in every way. Even when it gets hard, you must stay in there because you are a faithful soldier.

THE UNITY OF THE FAITH

Till we all come to the unity of the faith and of the knowledge of the Son of God, to a perfect man, to the measure of the stature of the fullness of Christ.

—Ephesians 4:13

You want to get to the place where God can use you, but He must win you over first. This happens as you migrate into places where you meet the people you need to connect with. You will grow and develop there because it is all about maturity and getting into the unity of the faith. That is the goal the Lord has for the body of Christ. That is why He sent the fivefold ministry to the church so that we would mature and be in the unity of the faith. If the fivefold is not developing you and bringing you into the unity of the faith, they are not doing what they are supposed to, and the body suffers. Each individual that does not do what they are supposed to do affects the rest of the body. √

The Holy Spirit in these days wants you to be around people of like faith. The fruit of the Spirit, the gifts of the Spirit, the fellowship and communion in the Spirit, taking communion together, and teaching will begin to operate when you do so. Being around people who value each other and feel safe and comfortable together is part of the *koinonia*[2] or the fellowship God wants for His people.

> *Therefore "'Come out from among them and be separate,' says the Lord. 'Do not touch what is unclean, and I will receive you.'"*   √
>
> 2 Corinthians 6:17

---

[2] "Lexicon :: Strong's G2842 – *koinonia*," Blue Letter Bible, accessed May 23, 2023, https://www.blueletterbible.org/lexicon/g2842/kjv/tr/0-1/.

In the cycles of the church, excitement cools down, and people get off track, but a remnant wants revival, a move of God. They want us to return to the original message of holiness, repentance, and the crucified life. All the great movements of God and the heroes that came out of them were marked by intense hunger for God. They wanted to be intimate with God, our Creator, in a hot spiritual atmosphere when it was cold all around them. Paul told the Corinthians to come out from among them and be separate. We already have this Scripture and the doctrine taught by the apostles that we are supposed to be following.

THE END-TIME CHURCH IS SUPPOSED TO BE HOT

That you may walk worthy of the Lord, fully pleasing Him, being fruitful in every good work and increasing in the knowledge of God; strengthened with all might, according to His glorious power, for all patience and longsuffering with joy.

—Colossians 1:10–11

The established church goes through these phases because we are in a fallen world, and those strong power words—words like the crucified life, repentance, holy fire, the blood of Jesus, and the name of Jesus—that the Lord gives us in Scripture are not emphasized. You will notice that the fivefold ministry no longer mentions certain truths, which is a telltale sign that we are under attack in the church. The end-time church is supposed to be hot. Unfortunately, persecution usually has to come in so that people decide whether it is worth it to follow God. The people who are dedicated and loyal to God cry out for Him to catch them on fire because they want to be hot and want more. These are the remnant.

We are going through that phase again, and as that remnant goes out, it grows because people start to do what they should have done all along. The telltale sign is that the church cools off, and attacks begin to increase. It starts with an onslaught of persecution, and rights are taken away. There may be a disease or war; something occurs so that people realize their peace has been affected. People then have to decide how they will respond. Will they ask God for help, or will they blame Him? Some people actually blame God when evil happens because they never mature into adults who can stand·against evil. The church is supposed to take authority and prevent corruption. God never wanted or sanctioned some of what is happening in the world, which is the church's fault.

When you see this happen, there will be a revelation phase where the Lord notices the people who have separated themselves unto

Him and strengthens them (Colossians 1:11). These people will receive revelation. They will see the truth in the Bible, all these power words, and start using them again. Then these believers will only want to be in services where they talk about Jesus all the time. They will speak of and pray in the name of Jesus; they will proclaim the blood of Jesus, the holy fire, the power of God, resurrection, raising the dead, healing the sick, and casting out devils.

You will see these small groups or pockets of people begin to form and grow because they have migrated out of the cold, ineffective church where they have stopped using the Word of God and the power words. Believers will want to leave that cold atmosphere and go to a hot church.

> *Whole countries have been touched by what began as a few people with a revelation that God had more for them than what they were experiencing.*

God will start visiting the services because of revelation, and it will become so strong that it becomes habitation. Lines of people will wait to get into the building for something that started as a Bible study or just a couple of people praying in the Spirit. That is how revivals start. Whole countries have been touched by what began as a few people with a revelation that God had more for them than what they were experiencing (Zechariah 4:9–10).

When it gets hot, you get healed and develop into a habitation of God. You get rid of trauma, discouragement, an orphan spirit, and a victim's spirit, and the demons start to leave because it's getting hot. As you increase in fellowship with these people, you will see that the holy fire is beginning to burn in the group instead of just one person.

The holy fire brings healing, and the demons start leaving because they have nothing to hold on to inside a group of people on fire. As soon as a person is healed, the demons lose their grip and leave. If the demons try to return, they find that person occupied by the Holy Spirit and healed. Since they dealt with their issues, the demons no longer have a hook within them (John 14:30). They cannot stay because the person matured from revelation into visitation into habitation, and there is no room for them anymore. That is where we are going with Warrior Notes and with Warrior Churches. We are developing a place where on-fire people gather together from all over the world.

WE ARE CALLED WITH A HOLY CALLING

People will receive supernatural healing because of the power in these meetings, which has already started happening. The power is so strong. When the demons are expelled, people's minds change, and they can no longer doubt or fear because the power and presence of God are with them. They are built up, having fellowship with one another and hearing the Word of God. They are strong, bold, and have friends who believe as they do. They feel comfortable, accepted, and valued, which is all part of the process.

As healings occur, the public shows an interest, and unsaved people begin to come. At first, these people are driven by curiosity; however, just like in the Book of Acts, the church will start to grow exponentially when they get saved, healed, and delivered. A repeat of the cycle happens every so often, and we are in it now. Many people realize they are in an ineffective, powerless, cold religion and probably don't understand what has happened.

> *And as you go, preach, saying, 'The kingdom of Heaven is at hand.' Heal the sick, cleanse the lepers, raise the dead, cast out demons. Freely you have received, freely give.*
>
> —Matthew 10:7–8

The Spirit of the Lord is upon Me, because He has anointed Me to preach the gospel to the poor; He has sent Me to heal the brokenhearted, to proclaim liberty to the captives and recovery of sight to the blind, to set at liberty those who are oppressed; to proclaim the acceptable year of the Lord.

—Luke 4:18–19

Many Christians are good people who have allowed the enemy to wear them down and out, shifting their focus from the message. The pure message of the gospel is that you heal the sick, raise the dead, drive out devils, and preach the year of Jubilee. The acceptable year of the Lord, Jubilee, is complete forgiveness of debt and sin.

Therefore if the Son makes you free, you shall be free indeed.

—John 8:36

As you preach the good news, you break the yokes off people, and the Spirit of the Lord gives freedom. As Christians, this is what we are called to do. But unfortunately, we go through cycles of becoming cold, then hot, and so forth. As believers, we should not go through cycles because we should always be hot, but it's a war down here.

Who has saved us and called us with a holy calling, not according to our works, but according to His own purpose and grace which was given to us in Christ Jesus before time began.

—2 Timothy 1:9

Think about what Paul told Timothy here and how everything was planned. Everything about the holy calling of God was completed according to His purpose and grace, given to us through Jesus Christ before time began. It was already planned. All the missing endowments we should have right now have already been predetermined in Christ. Before this world was ever formed, God, in His infinite knowledge, had already provided and planned all this.

I do not want you as a believer to go through the rest of your life not receiving what you have coming to you. Unfortunately, because of false and wrong teachings, people do not understand that it does not just come to you automatically. There is a process, and you must be tenacious and pursue God. God notices those who passionately pursue Him and rewards them for diligently seeking Him (Hebrews 11:6). However, if you do not diligently seek Him, He does not reward you.

> *We must remember that Jesus looked for people who were hungry and were pulling on Him.*

Jesus did not just pursue people. He answered them when they sought Him, then made Himself available to them, but He did not go out looking for people to minister to. We must remember that Jesus looked for people who were hungry and were pulling on Him.

Many Scriptures support the idea that we must actively and aggressively seek Jesus and move toward Him (Jeremiah 29:12–13; Matthew 6:33; Luke 11:9–13; Hebrews 11:6; James 4:8). God favors those who are diligently seeking Him and favor Him. They catch God's eye, and He wants to strengthen them (2 Chronicles 16:9). When I studied church history through the ages and from my vantage point after visiting Jesus in Heaven, I can tell you that God does not do this for everyone, only for those who pursue Him.

God wants to favor and strengthen every person and make these blessings available to all but not everyone takes Him up on it. No one should go to hell, but people are dying and going to hell every second. It is unnecessary because Jesus died for them and has an amazing plan, yet people perish, but it is not God's perfect will. I do not want you to finish your life without knowing what is available; I want you to understand and participate in His revealed will. God has many wonderful things for those who love Him and are called according to His purpose (Romans 8:28).

WATCH AND PRAY YOU WILL NOT FALL INTO TEMPTATION

Keep actively watching and praying that you may not come into temptation; the spirit is willing, but the body is weak.

—Matthew 26:41 AMP

If everything was automatically given to you, why would Jesus say this? Why would He tell the disciples to keep watching and praying so they do not fall into temptation? From this, we can see that you can fall into temptation, and if you don't do anything, you *will* fall into temptation. You have to be actively watching and praying. The critical point that many miss is that the Spirit is willing, which is why they become lukewarm. The Holy Spirit in your spirit is on fire, and He is always ready.

When your spirit is born again, it is a new creation in Christ (2 Corinthians 5:17). The old is gone, and your spirit is ready and willing. You are as prepared as you are ever going to be in your spirit, and the Holy Spirit is in there with you, and He is willing. However, the flesh is unredeemed, weak, and struggling, fighting against God and you—this is happening to many now.

The faith in people's hearts is not strong enough to overcome the mind and the flesh, and because people are not being fed spiritually in churches, the flesh becomes stronger. In order to appease people and keep them, many churches appeal to their souls and emotions. In these churches, you will hear what we call feel-good messages. They will talk about sports and entertainment, sprinkled with all these stories about fun things that appeal to your flesh and emotions. Unfortunately, those ministers rob the people and God because they are responsible for feeding a person's spirit, lighting them up for God, and fanning the fire within them.

Revelation, visitation, and habitation will first bring the holy fire and then the harvest. People need to be delivered. You cannot feed your flesh and soul and think that demons will be expelled or people will be healed. You must increase the atmosphere of Heaven, which means you will have to feed your spirit.

We must allow the Holy Spirit to speak through us. The gospel is a message of the good news; as Jesus said, it is raising the dead, preaching Jubilee (debt cancellation) and the resurrection power of

Jesus, expelling demons, and healing the sick. We must preach the good news that God is good and Jesus is coming back again.

8

BE SPIRIT-RULED

Who will also confirm you to the end, that you may be
blameless in the day of our Lord Jesus Christ.
—1 Corinthians 1:8

Jesus explained that we need to be led by the Holy Spirit, Who will lead us into all truth (John 16:13). Be sure to be led by the Spirit; if you want the truth, then the Spirit is truth. If you want to be on fire, the Holy Spirit is fire. It is all about the Spirit of God. The Spirit will give you gifts from God and implement them in your life. Everything else will go well because the Lord will manage your life physically and mentally if *you* diligently tend to your spiritual life (Matthew 6:33).

I encourage you to ask the Holy Spirit to reveal Himself to you, ask Him to visit you, then ask Him to inhabit you. This process will expel the demonic that is coming against you. It will heal you from traumatic events and hurts that happened when you were younger, which you do not understand. God wants to heal you of all those traumas and rid you of any place where a devil can abide in your emotions or thoughts; He wants to deliver you.

REFUSE EVERY FORM OF EVIL

Abstain from every form of evil. Now may the God of peace Himself sanctify you completely; and may your whole spirit, soul, and body be preserved blameless at the coming of our Lord Jesus Christ.

—1 Thessalonians 5:22–23

Paul explained to the church at Thessalonica how God created them with three parts, which will help you to understand yourself. Many people do not know why they oppose themselves within themselves, and it is because we are made up of these three different areas. We were created in a very complex manner because we were supposed to operate at a higher level and a higher realm, but because we fell, we are in this broken world. It is challenging to function here because we were not made to deal with all this stress, disappointment, and discouragement. We were not created to have a separation of the physical, mental, and spiritual realms.

Paul tells us to abstain from every form of evil, so we are supposed to put a stop to evil and evil spirits. Then Paul asks that the God of peace sanctify you completely, and that word *sanctify*[3] means "to set apart." Then he asks that your whole spirit, soul, and body—those three different parts—be preserved blameless at the coming of our Lord Jesus Christ. So it is possible for us to be blameless. Three different words are used here in the original language. The soul is not the same as the spirit; people will try to combine or interchange these words, but they are different parts of us.

GETTING YOUR SOUL TO AGREE WITH YOUR SPIRIT

Your spirit is the real you that will live eternally, which can be born again by the Holy Spirit. Then you have your soul, which includes your mind, will, and emotions, which has to be renewed (Ephesians 4:23–24). Your mind must be transformed and renewed by the Word of God (Romans 12:2). So your soul must be corrected. It must be given the correct information so you can manage your thoughts and

---

[3] "Lexicon :: Strong's G37 – *hagiazō* ," Blue Letter Bible, accessed May 23, 2023, https://www.blueletterbible.org/lexicon/g37/kjv/tr/0-1/.

emotions based on the Word of God. Finally, your *body* needs to be disciplined. Paul said that after he preached Christ, he would be disqualified from his race if he did not discipline his body (1 Corinthians 9:27).

Paul said his body, if left undisciplined, could cause him to get off track and lose out (1 Corinthians 9:27). Your body will do what it wants if you let it, and your soul, which is your mind, will, and emotions, can also derail you. However, when your spirit is born again, it becomes a new creation (2 Corinthians 5:17). Your spirit is where you rule and reign. From your spirit, you can tell your soul what to think and feel and your body what to do. This truth is evident in Scripture, especially in chapter 8 of Romans.

It is possible to be spirit-ruled instead of body-ruled. It is also possible to be spirit-ruled rather than governed by your thoughts and emotions, which may be right or wrong. Your body, mind, will, and emotions are inconsistent in their behavior; however, your born-again heart, your spirit that is ruling and reigning inside you, is steadfast. If you are not born again, you are in trouble because you are powerless to say no to ungodliness. You have no power to say no to the prince of the power of the air and have no resistance to him whatsoever (Ephesians 2:1–3). As a believer, you must get people born again.

You need to pray in the Holy Spirit, building yourself up in your most holy faith in your spirit as a spiritual exercise (Jude 1:20). You must renew your mind by the Word of God and discipline your body, telling it what it can and cannot do. You will constantly have to do this during your journey on earth.

> *So that you come short in no gift, eagerly waiting for the revelation of our Lord Jesus Christ, Who will also confirm you to the end, that you may be blameless in the day of our Lord Jesus Christ.*
>
> —1 Corinthians 1:7–8

Once again, Paul is telling the Corinthians, who were carnal, that they can be blameless because God wants to establish them to the end. God wants to continually interact with you and confirm you, which is what having a relationship with Him is all about. This is the kind of relationship we are supposed to have with the Lord, where we allow Him to come in and influence us.

PUTTING THE WORD OF GOD BEFORE YOUR EYES, EARS, AND MOUTH

As you think, work through, and manage yourself in all these situations, you are essentially building up your spirit. You renew your mind by studying the Word of God and build yourself up in your spirit by praying in tongues (Romans 12:2; Jude 1:20). As you meditate on the Word of God, your mind, will, and emotions change into a framework that represents what the Word of God says. Essentially, you are getting your soul to agree with your spirit, which takes the surrender of your entire life.

> *I know the only way I will be effective is if my life is wholly saturated with God's presence.*

You can accelerate this process if you are totally immersed in an environment where you hear, see, and say the Lord's will for your life. That is why we have all the media available at Warrior Notes. Then, we have the conferences so that you get together with other people under a corporate anointing where you are saturated and completely immersed in God's presence. In my personal life, I do this all the time, not just at conferences. I not only want to walk in overthrow, but I also want to live in it. I know the only way I will be effective is if my life is wholly saturated with God's presence.

And all of us, as with unveiled face, [because we] continued to behold [in the Word of God] as in a mirror the glory of the Lord, are constantly being transfigured into His very own image in ever increasing splendor and from one degree of glory to another; [for this comes] from the Lord [Who is] the Spirit.

—2 Corinthians 3:18 AMPC

You need to put the Word of God before your eyes, ears, and mouth, and then you hit the devil in all those different areas. When that happens, your mind changes, which is what repentance is. You may experience a sudden breakthrough; however, remember that your soul is being saved continually (Philippians 2:12). You go from glory to glory as your soul is being saved, whereas your spirit is already saved. Your soul is being saved because it is being renewed. The change is coming because your perceptions are changing, causing you to ascend to a higher vantage point.

DISCIPLINING YOUR BODY

Your body just needs to get used to discipline. For example, if you exercise every day at a specific time, it becomes routine. I used to run every day at a certain time. It was amazing because ten minutes before running, I would start feeling my blood flowing with adrenaline and energy, and I would start to feel my circulation and energy increase. When I looked at the clock, I realized I was due to go on my run. My body had gotten used to going for that four or sometimes eight-mile run. My body was subconsciously tuned into that run every day to where everything my body needed for that run was already being pumped into my bloodstream beforehand. This took no conscious effort on my part; it was happening because I had disciplined my body to exercise at a specific time every day for years.

It was the same when I attended college for four years. After class, I rested and had dinner, and then I disciplined my body to study all night to ensure I could pass the coming tests. This way of life became commonplace and was not something I had to try to do. I just disciplined myself. It was not fun when I first started, but it got to where it was just part of my daily routine, and this is how it should be with us as Christians. It should be natural to speak to God when you wake up in the morning. Proclaim the Word of God, pray in the Spirit, and then go about your day, doing whatever you are supposed to do.

When you get used to doing things a certain way, it becomes a part of you and is automatic. As a student of the Lord, you take all these courses and are studying, being diligent, and understanding different subjects. Then when you are talking to people, you might automatically say, "Well, it says here in Romans chapter twelve that we are supposed to present our bodies as a living sacrifice, and this will help us know the perfect will of God." You will start to flow naturally with the things of God. All your studying, taking courses, and daily routine with the Lord will pay off because it becomes part of you and flows out of you.

Isn't it amazing how people have certain skills? Though very talented, professional athletes and musicians still have to practice constantly. You think, *Oh, my gosh, how could I ever do that?* But those professionals thought the same thing at one time. They just started to do it all the time. Studies have been done on specific sports that found that if you do them twice a week, you will only maintain the level you have already reached. However, if you go to that third time, that third day, that third practice, you will start to excel.

I applied to be a flight instructor at an airport school during my off time. They said they would hire me, but I needed to consider a particular detail. They knew I had been working with an airline I loved for over a year, and I was often on trips. They said they needed me to commit to their students flying with me at least twice a week and possibly three times because of that study. They knew that a student was required to practice two or three times a week to improve, so they wanted me to be available. I only worked three days a week at my job because I worked twelve-hour days. I could work a whole week in three days, so I was also available to take their flight instructor job.

My point with those examples is that it is the same with God's Word and your walk with Him. If you make prayer and studying His Word part of your daily routine, it becomes part of you. You do not even have to think about it anymore. When people desired to advance in any profession and started practicing for five and six days a week, they excelled exponentially and passed everyone. They went far beyond people who practiced only two or three times a week.

EXCEL IN THE THINGS OF GOD

Be encouraged that God will present you blameless to Him, but the process of how you excel and the level you reach is really up to you, and there is no limit. I know this to be true. Yes, you will go to Heaven because you have accepted Jesus. And yes, God will use you because you are studying and diligent. But how far you go and how much you are allowed to know is more up to you than you might like to admit. In other words, if you submit yourself to the Holy Spirit every day and ask Him to teach you, that will take you further and probably faster than someone who sits and reads their Bible once a week and then goes to church and listens to a sermon.

> *In this life, there are no limits, but it is up to you. You have to choose to saturate yourself in God.*

If you go and listen to a sermon, that helps. If you open your Bible once a week, that helps, and if you pray a prayer before you eat, that helps. What about waking up and praying for an hour, reading your Bible, then praying and reading your Bible at night before you go to bed? Then during the day, pray in the Spirit quietly to yourself, even while you are at work or out doing errands. Then have a Scripture card, which is one verse you chose for that day, and keep reviewing that during the day. I have done this over the years, which has helped me grow personally, and I will not hide or keep that secret from you.

In this life, there are no limits, but it is up to you. You have to choose to saturate yourself in God. If everyone else is doing ten minutes of spiritual activity a day, like reading the Bible or praying, and you were to do that twice a day, essentially, you would be doing double what they are doing. If you extend that to ten minutes every two hours and add to that praying silently in the Spirit while you are at work, can you imagine exponentially what that will do for your spiritual life? Imagine how you will develop spiritually over the years. You will be a spiritual giant and be able to weather anything, no matter what.

Right now, I see so many hungry people who want the supernatural. They want to be hot. They want to be in the holy fire constantly. They want to be able to handle not just revelation and visitation but habitation. They want to see the harvest come in. They want to create an atmosphere where people are saved, healed, and delivered, where it is not just casual. If you want that, it will take a commitment from you of more than just ten minutes a day; you will have to take time throughout your day to find a way to look at your Scripture card and pray silently in the Spirit. You can find a way to work this into your schedule and make it part of your life.

I am firmly convinced that I do not want to be labeled as just a Christian. I want to be a believer. You know a believer by their actions. Others do not have to tell you that person is a believer. I can feel faith around people when they have faith and holy fire when they have it. I can tell, but it is not from what they tell me—I can sense it and see it. It is a reality. It is an environment. The Holy Spirit is very willing right now to take you into this, but it must be a lifestyle.

Some people will come against believers with high standards. I guess people feel they can come against people enforcing a higher standard because if they get rid of that standard, they can live with lower standards and do not feel convicted. Unfortunately, this happens when believers take a stand for righteousness and justice; people want to get rid of them. People will try to chip away at you and say you are extreme, but we need hot people. We need people in the holy fire, set apart and saturated with God, because we need healing, deliverance, debt cancellation, and the harvest to come in. These will not come from lukewarm Christians but from white-hot, Spirit-filled believers that have saturated themselves with the environment of Heaven.

I will not hold back from you, and I am telling you all the secrets I know because I believe you want to know them. I have done these things for the last forty years and have invested in my spiritual life constantly. Even if it is in secret, you have to do it. People had no idea what I was doing all those years I was at work. They did not understand, even though it was happening the whole time. The Lord was preparing me over those thirty years at my job. The entire time I was there, my spiritual life was developing, even though I was working and doing what I needed for my company. In reality, I was preparing for what we are doing now.

I believe that God has put us all together and that we will excel in the things God has for us. It is never too late to grasp what you are supposed to be doing. You can go way beyond the norm others have settled for and start right now. I want you to excel in the things of God.

9

DESTROYING BARRIERS

Now when they saw the boldness of Peter and John, and
perceived that they were uneducated
and untrained men, they marveled. And they realized
that they had been with Jesus.
—Acts 4:13

A time must come when you face the issues in your life and allow God to heal you. It's time to flip the tables on the enemy. God did not do the hurtful things that happened to you because that is not His nature. Many people secretly blame God for allowing them to get hurt, but we are in a fallen world and have free will. The church is not teaching this, so there is confusion. Many people do not understand that God is not always going to step in and stop sin.

I have stopped people from dying on their deathbeds because I refused to let them die. It was not because I cried; I did not shed one tear, and it had nothing to do with my emotions. I did not even physically do anything except say, "No, no, it is not their time." I found people who would agree with me, and we saw a huge turnaround; I have seen it happen many times. However, you cannot think a breakthrough is based on your emotions or the tears you shed and believe God will respond to that; He responds to faith. You also cannot think that whatever happens is God's will, and then when something terrible happens, you blame God. That thinking goes against the fact that God is a good God; He doesn't kill, steal, or destroy.

THE DEVIL COMES TO STEAL, KILL, AND DESTROY

The thief does not come except to steal, and to kill, and to destroy. I have come that they may have life, and that they may have it more abundantly.

—John 10:10

If you are experiencing theft or destruction, the devil is doing that. Jesus went around doing good and healing everyone who was oppressed by the devil. God is good, and so He does good. Jesus said that the thief steals, kills, and destroys; Jesus gives life more abundantly. I judge if God is working by asking if this is abundant life. If there is abundant life, then that is Jesus. If stealing, killing, and destroying happen, I know exactly where that is coming from— the devil.

Look what happened in the book of Job as soon as the devil was permitted to attack Job (Job 1:6–12). All the evil that came against him had to do with the enemy armies operating through the weather, disease, killing, stealing, and destroying. Job's family and livestock were killed. You can see all the avenues that satan used against Job as soon as satan was told he could do it. The enemy even influenced his wife, who said to Job, "Curse God and die" (Job 2:9). The devil spoke through her. Even his neighbors came against him. Knowing this helps us understand how satan operates against us.

BUILT UP IN THE SPIRIT AND HAVING A COMMAND ABOUT YOU

Overthrow comes when you settle in, and all that chaff has been burned out of your life. All the barriers caused by blaming God for what has happened are gone. You have stopped asking yourself things like, *Why did God let that happen? I asked God to help me, and He didn't. I asked God to heal me. Why didn't He?* Did you ever think you had to drive devils out by being diligent and putting your foot down? You needed to say, "No, I am going to live and not die and declare the works of the Lord. I will be in the land of the living. I am going to prosper. I will not be in debt anymore" (Psalm 118:17).

My wife and I spent seven years speaking, standing, and fighting against debt before we got out of debt. It wasn't because I was crying, and it wasn't because I was trying. It wasn't because I was casually coming at it either. No. My wife and I aggressively came against debt for seven years. Nothing happened in the first three years we went after it, but we stayed aggressive, and then the overthrow happened. You must understand that you cannot appeal to God in your emotions or throw out a half-hearted prayer now and then, like you pray before you eat. There are different types of prayer.

If the issue is life and death and it has to do with demonic spirits, you must be diligent and aggressive; you must have a command about yourself. You also have to be built up in the Spirit. As soon as God reveals something to you, every single time, every demon in hell will come against you to steal that very revelation that has been given to you. As soon as you get an idea from God, as soon as you are shown God's intention, satan will try to ensure that it doesn't happen. The enemy will try to make you look like a fool; satan will try to make everything about your dream from God and what He said to you look as if it will never happen. The enemy will start to kill, steal, and destroy to get rid of that vision, that seed that God planted in you.

Why does the enemy take so much effort to come against God's will for you? If God brings Heaven to earth, it will not just change you; it will change other people because you will not keep quiet about it. You will tell everyone that you believed in God, and He came through. Once you get a bunch of people together believing, it creates momentum. Then satan will start losing people, and you know he does not want to lose anyone he has entrapped. Think about all the multitudes that went to hear Jesus as He ministered. Those people were not going to the synagogues or the temple, so you can imagine what the Pharisees thought. No one was coming to ask them questions or coming to the temple to worship anymore.

Multitudes went out to listen to this Jesus talk. The Bible tells us what the people were saying about Him. "No man has ever spoken like this Man" (John 7:46). Others observed that He spoke with such authority, unlike the Pharisees (Mark 1:22). You can see that people had turned and were no longer listening to the religious system. The Pharisees and religious leaders, who were under the influence of demonic spirits, came at Jesus because those spirits were keeping people in bondage through the religious system.

> *For men will be lovers of themselves, lovers of money, boasters, proud, blasphemers, disobedient to parents, unthankful, unholy, unloving, unforgiving, slanderers, without self-control, brutal, despisers of good, traitors, headstrong, haughty, lovers of pleasure rather than lovers of God, having a form of godliness but denying its power. And from such people turn away!*
>
> —2 Timothy 3:2–5

Today, many religious churches and people have a form of godliness but deny the power thereof. What if the devil is using religion to keep people lukewarm, in bondage, and spiritually starving? What if these dead, dry churches are causing people to question, "Is this all there is?" These are the same churches that are not mentioning the subjects that make devils tremble. They do not talk about anything that will turn on the holy fire in your life or even tell you that you need to be separate from the world.

> *When the church becomes lukewarm, people decide we need to return to the subjects that can destroy hell so that people are saved, healed, and delivered again.*

The Pharisees came after Jesus. Every demon in hell will come after you if you stand for the truth and speak that truth to others because of the momentum that it creates. At the end of three-and-a-half years, they killed Jesus because He had such a huge following. Thousands of people were following Him, which started a whole movement. They began to call them Christians because the believers acted like Jesus Christ, and they noted that those people had been with Jesus (Acts 4:13). They turned the world upside down. The church was birthed in the book of Acts and grew until we have this body of believers today.

When the church becomes lukewarm, people decide we need to return to the subjects that can destroy hell so that people are saved, healed, and delivered again. That religious cycle is essentially the lukewarm church, and people started coming out of it. Denominations are formed from moves of God, and they eventually become cold; then, movements come out of the denominations. This cycle seems to repeat itself every hundred years or so.

Jesus came speaking the truth, and they killed Him for it. He had such a following that even when they killed Him, it caused an increase, and then the Holy Spirit came (Acts 2). Now God gives you vision as He speaks to you and starts to heal you. You finally realize God didn't do those terrible things to you. He wasn't even permitting them; He was just not invited into your life and those situations. In Heaven, I saw many things I had allowed to happen in my past, whether through negligence or ignorance. It didn't matter. God only comes into situations when He is invited.

When Jesus was invited into situations, He helped; however, He did not go out looking for people to heal. Instead, people came to Him. Jesus ministered to people because they were lost sheep and knew they needed a shepherd. He did not go out looking for disciples. He had twelve chosen disciples and sent out seventy-two others (Luke 10:1–2). Jesus went places, and people came and sat and listened to Him talk, and then they were healed and delivered. It is like this today; Jesus waits for us to invite Him in.

AUTHORITY TO BECOME CHILDREN OF GOD

Jesus could not heal anyone in His hometown because people were not asking for help. They saw Jesus as the carpenter's son and failed to see Him as the Messiah (Mark 6:1–6). Jesus said He could not heal in His hometown due to their unbelief. Religious organizations have grown cold today and do not discern the Lord for who He is. As we read in 2 Chronicles 16:9, the Lord is looking to and fro for anyone who has passionately grabbed onto Him and honors Him, and He will strengthen those people. The Lord wants to dwell with those who have a contrite and humble spirit (Isaiah 57:15).

> *But those who embraced Him and took hold of His name He gave authority to become the children of God!*
>
> —John 1:12 TPT

Many people do not understand this about God, but they need to; He wants to be invited into situations.

Jesus gave authority to those who actively reached out and embraced Him, and they became children of God. It was the same way with the parables. When the disciples came to Jesus and said they did not understand the parable, Jesus would sit with them and explain it. They could not understand why He did not explain it to everyone. Jesus answered and said to them, "Because it has been given to you to know the mysteries of the kingdom of heaven, but to them, it has not been given" (Matthew 13:11). Jesus would not tell the public but shared with the disciples; that is how it is with God. Many people do not understand this about God, but they need to; He wants to be invited into situations.

Corrupt governments are all over the world because the people and the church have not invited God in. An overthrow needs to happen in the spirit realm, but the people don't ask for it. God said He would not destroy Sodom and Gomorrah if He found ten righteous people (Genesis 18:32). A big enough group of righteous people needs to talk to God, negotiate, and say, "Lord, this is not like You to do this, and we need you to work with us." Moses, Abraham, and David were all able to talk to God, and they came to an agreement with Him. They covenanted together with Him because they invited Him into their situation, which is what we need to do. You must actively reach out and ask God to help you.

THE TENACITY TO ENFORCE OVERTHROW

Most people today are hurt and mad at God because they think He let certain situations happen to them when they were a child. They feel that they asked God, and He did not do anything about it, but God will not necessarily answer an emotional prayer. The Father wants you to operate in sonship and as His friend. When you are not born again or not developed in maturity, you do not know how to pray or even know the different types of prayers to pray. Still, no matter what level you are operating on, God will help you the best that He can in that situation.

I had the revelation that we can permit things to happen. It might be that we did nothing about it, and that was enough for the devil to come in. That is what I saw, and I am telling you the truth. I don't know how else to tell people this, but we are supposed to take certain actions, or nothing will be done. History will show that many interventions should have taken place, but never happened. Wickedness is supposed to be overturned and blocked through us, but this will not be done if we do not do something about it.

You may pray for something to be done, and then God will elect *you* to do it. However, if you disobey or say you will do it and don't follow through, it will not be done. Those who prayed could say that they prayed and it did not happen, but God answered their prayer by telling someone (maybe them) to do it. If a person does not obey God, it will not be done. In some situations, God went through many people before He found one willing to do it. Think about that. How many people do you think God had to go through before He found a Kathryn Kuhlman or a Smith Wigglesworth? What about something you asked four years ago that still hasn't happened? Yet God might have asked eight people, and none would do it.

A point has to come in your life where you resolve the lie that God caused or allowed hurtful situations in your past. Some circumstances happened because you did not understand and were not actively pursuing God, asking Him to come into the situation. As we grow up, we must let go of those lies and realize that the devil is mean and we are in a fallen world. The devil is the god of this world, and often, God does not have His way. However, God can now have His way because you invite Him in and have become mature enough to take a stand.

I want you to get into the place where you have the tenacity to enforce overthrow. You ask, and you know that you receive; you seek, and you know you will find; you knock, and you know the door will be opened to you (Matthew 7:7). When Jesus spoke those instructions, He approached them differently than most of us have understood. It was as though He were saying, "You know you will receive when you ask, you know the door will be opened when you knock, and you know that you will find if you seek. Period."

Therefore I say to you, whatever things you ask when you pray, believe that you receive them, and you will have them.

—Mark 11:24

Jesus said that if you pray, believing that you receive it, you *will* have it. You must understand you already got it before you even ask, that is getting into overthrow. A sign of maturity, a sign that you are receiving and operating as a son or daughter of God, is that you don't hesitate. It's the same as when you train your body; you reach a point where it becomes a lifestyle without hesitation. Athletes make sports look so easy, but it is because they have done it for years, and it just looks seamless. That is how it is even in your spiritual life. When you encounter the devil, you should be so quick to respond and react that you even surprise the devil by taking care of it immediately.

Did you know that you can surprise the devil? The devil and his demons flip out over people in overthrow. They flip out because they see you have no hesitation or fear. God wants to mature you because today, we need warriors, people well-trained in spiritual matters to bring in the harvest and build up the body of Christ. When overthrow happens, it is because you have been delivered and healed inside your heart.

The traumatic events that happened to you were valid; you trusted people and were a victim. You now know these events occurred because we are in an imperfect, fallen world. However, you are no longer where you were and now understand truth you did not understand before. You are now in a new place spiritually; you are growing every day, and the devils know it. The devil and his demons know they can no longer operate against you, so they will try to stop your momentum. You will understand how to eliminate the ability of the evil spirits to get to you; the Holy Spirit will show you how to do it and seal it up for you.

10

ENFORCING OVERTHROW

Moreover whom He predestined, these He also called;
whom He called, these He also justified; and whom He
justified, these He also glorified.
—Romans 8:30

As we discussed, many things happened to you when you were younger because you were not where you are now and did not understand everything you do now. However, you cannot blame God, and you cannot blame others. You must forgive. Forgiveness releases you from the responsibility of dealing with those matters yourself. Forgiveness is a legal case turned over to God; when you forgive, you are, in reality, handing the whole matter over to Him so He can take care of it. Some people think that if you forgive someone, that exonerates them; no, it releases *you*. You do it for your own spiritual well-being, so release everything. People do not get away with sin just because you forgive them. God will handle it.

GOD WILL DIRECT YOUR PATHS

I do not blame God nor do I blame anything on anyone. I take full responsibility for where I am today, understanding that I can experience a reset and go on to be very productive for the rest of my life. So I will not blame people, circumstances, or God. If you meet Jesus, it will take you forever to get up enough guts even to say something to Him. Never mind telling Him that He was wrong or confronting Him by saying, "Why did this happen?" You will never say that, and you will never be able to blame Him because He is not at fault. Jesus is not wrong, has never been wrong, and will never apologize.

Jesus has given us everything we need for life and godliness, as Peter said (2 Peter 1:3). Jesus has done everything He is going to do about the devil and everything He is going to do about healing. He has already suffered and died, made a show of the devil openly, and provided for us (Colossians 2:15). You will find that out when you get to Heaven. When people pursue God and acknowledge Him in all their ways, He directs their paths because they engage God and include Him (Proverbs 3:6).

YOU SHOULD ALREADY KNOW WHAT GOD LIKES AND DISLIKES

Will a man rob God? Yet you have robbed Me! But you say, 'In what way have we robbed You?' In tithes and offerings.

—Malachi 3:8

During Malachi's day, God asked, "Will a man rob God?" The people neglected what they had already been told because they were supposed to be tithing. As a result, God let them face problems until they finally asked the Lord what was happening, and Malachi prophesied that God said they were robbing Him. When they asked God how they were robbing Him, He told them, "In tithes and offerings," and then they repented. It is sad because people who follow God should already know what God likes and does not like.

These six things the Lord hates, yes, seven are an abomination to Him: a proud look, a lying tongue, hands that shed innocent blood, a heart that devises wicked plans, feet that are swift in running to evil, a false witness who speaks lies, and one who sows discord among brethren.

—Proverbs 6:16–19

In the Bible, God says there are seven things He hates; if He hates them, you should hate them too. If God likes certain things, you should like them. Unfortunately, these truths slip away from us. When you reach Heaven, you will realize that you should have known and practiced all these, which I found out. I discovered they were all true even when I didn't think about or understand them. Even if I had known and ignored these, I still would have robbed myself and others because I could have been more productive. I will never find myself in that situation again. I will be fruitful for the rest of my life because I know I cannot lose.

WE ARE THE GLORIOUS CHURCH

I realize I could stop ministering right now and be fine; however, I choose not to because I know too much. It is all rigged in my favor if I obey the Lord; God has already provided all that I need and defeated the devil, having made a show of him openly. So it does not matter if it looks like the enemy is taking over the earth. God has us, His glorious church, on the earth, and the gates of hell cannot prevail against us (Matthew 16:18). We must stay in there and remember what God has already said.

> *You will realize that you cannot fail and are not a victim; then, you can turn and start to help others, which is the fulfillment of the body.*

Once you are delivered, you will realize all that Jesus has done and become comfortable with that. You will realize that you cannot fail and are not a victim; then, you can turn and start to help others, which is the fulfillment of the body. We should be ministering to each other, not just ourselves. Ministering only to yourself is the mentality of a victim and a sign you are in survival mode and want to self-preserve. The rich young ruler was operating in self-preservation, and Jesus was trying to get him out of that mode. Jesus told him to sell everything he had and give it to the poor, and he would have treasure in Heaven. Then, Jesus said to come and follow Him (Matthew 19:21).

The rich young ruler could not obey and follow Jesus because he was a victim, an orphan, in survival mode. Unfortunately, we meet wonderful people all the time with a victim mentality or who are just surviving, trying to preserve themselves. It is almost like they are in a chess game and trying to position themselves so they come out ahead. They are always strategizing, which is not how we should be as believers.

BELIEVERS IN OVERTHROW SHOCK DEMONS

A believer is supposed to turn everything over to God. You are not a victim, not an orphan, not abandoned, and not rejected. Let God accept you, love on you, prosper you, and bless you with good health (3 John 1:2). Build yourself up and get to the place where you are in overthrow so you can see the devil chased out of town. The demons are shocked when a person is in overthrow because they do not see that many people reach the point of walking in who they are in Christ.

When you realize who you are, you know it is not about pushing your position; you are who you are and do not have to defend yourself. You never have to prove yourself to anyone or apologize for who you are. You are who you are because God is who He is. You identify with Him, He identifies with you, and you walk in a close relationship with Him.

Believers in overthrow shock demons, who operate throughout the earth to keep people in a victim or rejection mode. The demons do not know what to do with someone not in victim, orphan, or rejection mode because none of their schemes work on them. You will see demons pushing and pressuring these people, but it is counterproductive because all they do is run to God, get into the glory, and get ignited. When the demons see that their plan isn't working and the opposite is happening, they back off and leave these people alone. They do not know what to do with a person who is thoroughly convinced of their God and who is not responding out of their emotions or mind but out of their spirit. You become like a fine-tuned machine because you have allowed the Holy Spirit to develop you.

SAVED BY FAITH, NOT BY WORKS

For by grace you have been saved through faith, and that not of yourselves; it is the gift of God, not of works, lest anyone should boast.

—Ephesians 2:8–9

The religious system is like a crutch because it teaches you to rely on man, programs, formulas, etc. They tell you that this or that will happen if you say specific prayers or commit to certain church doctrines. I was told I would go to Heaven if I joined the church, was baptized, and behaved for the rest of my life. I thought, *Okay, I have to join the church, be sprinkled with water, and be a good person for the rest of my life. Then God will decide if I make it into Heaven.* I had no assurance I would go to Heaven even if I did what the church told me to do. Then I discovered that I was saved not by works but by faith and that I needed to be born again.

My former pastor never mentioned the born-again experience and Jesus's name. He mentioned God but never Jesus, and I do not remember him talking about anything spiritual. When I asked him questions, he did not even know the answer. When I became born again, I was very upset because I felt the religious system kept me out instead of bringing me in. Since I was born again at nineteen, I have spent my whole life on this journey of discovery and learning the truth that the Bible teaches.

> *However, when He, the Spirit of truth, has come, He will guide you into all truth; for He will not speak on His own authority, but whatever He hears He will speak; and He will tell you things to come. He will glorify Me, for He will take of what is Mine and declare it to you.*
>
> —John 16:13–14

I found that the Holy Spirit was given to reveal the truth, which I was never taught. I was never told that the Holy Spirit is a Person Who is inside you and is teaching, leading, and guiding you; He is our friend. I was not taught that He is with us now or how to pray properly. I had a victim mentality and felt rejected and orphaned even when I was around people and in church two or three times a week. I was tithing, doing good works, and doing my best, but it did not help me overcome the evil that was working. Spiritual warfare was going on, and I knew it, but I could not do anything about it.

When I was born again, I was ignited and activated and started gaining awareness that I needed more understanding. I learned more about the Bible by spending time with people who believed in being born again, yet they did not understand warfare or what to do about the devil. They did not teach the in-Him doctrine that Paul taught in Ephesians 2:4–9, which is about being in Christ, the benefits of being in Jesus, and being seated with Him in the heavenly places. None of that was taught. I had to move out of that place and go where they were always teaching about being in Christ.

FINDING THE HOLY FIRE AND WHERE
GOD IS MOVING

As I searched for where God was moving, each step I took worked for a while, but then I noticed that people around me started growing cold, and the message started to change. At first, the leaders seemed to be doing the same godly works, but the results were not the same. I realized it was not heartfelt anymore, then I had to move again. I had to go out and find where God was moving and where the fire was. It forced me into this place of holy fire where I had to let the Lord work on me. I was called to be a standard-bearer, a leader who would operate in faith, calling things that were not as they were (Romans 4:17).

> *Yet in all these things we are more than conquerors through Him who loved us.*
>
> —Romans 8:37

> *I realized my future was secure; all I had to do was be diligent down here and stay hot.*

I got to where I knew the end was secure because when I died, I saw the end, and then I was sent back. I realized my future was secure; all I had to do was be diligent down here and stay hot. I was called to remain on fire and enforce the victory already given to me when I saw into the future. When I came back, I saw that I was more than a conqueror and that I was in overthrow. That was because I already saw I had made it to the end. I saw all the saints in Heaven that were ever going to live, every one of them that was ever born, and probably some that are not in existence yet.

In Heaven, I saw the end, which has not even happened yet on earth, but has already happened there. Then I was sent back. God told me, "Here is where you are going, and now I want you to be part of this." So here I am, and with everything we are doing, I essentially enforce victory and overthrow. It has already happened, yet I watch it unfold in this realm. It is slower, and in some cases, it has not happened yet, but I know it will. I am enforcing what God showed me about the future. I am not concerned about what people are worried about because I know it is already taken care of.

JESUS IS SEATED IN HEAVEN, WAITING FOR HIS ENEMIES TO BECOME HIS FOOTSTOOL

And we know that all things work together for good to those who love God, to those who are the called according to His purpose. For whom He foreknew,

He also predestined to be conformed to the image of His Son, that He might be the firstborn among many brethren. Moreover whom He predestined, these He also called; whom He called, these He also justified; and whom He justified, these He also glorified.

—Romans 8:28–30

In the book of Romans, Paul shares many insights and gives us extensive revelation. After His ascension, we know that Jesus Christ went to and remains in the timeless realm, our future; He is now seated at the right hand of God (Hebrews 12:2). Jesus is seated because He has accomplished everything He is going to perform and is now waiting for His enemies to become His footstool through the church (Hebrews 10:12–13). Jesus took captivity captive, ascended on high, and distributed gifts to everyone (Ephesians 4:7–10). Jesus took what He had won, distributed it among the body, and sat down. Now Jesus waits, but it is not *waiting* like we think because there is no time.

Time does not pass in Heaven like it does down here. There is no calendar. It is not like we have tomorrow, then we have off, or we have the weekend. It's not like vacation is coming next month. It is not like that with God. He is the I Am, and nothing bothers Him. There is no time in Heaven, so for God, it is already done, and waiting is nothing to Him. It could be a thousand years down here, which is a day up there (2 Peter 3:8). Time passes down here, yet nothing has happened on His timetable, because He is waiting for His enemies to become His footstool through the church.

So satan throws out these ideas to the body and the world that we are waiting on God. However, that is false. The world says that if God wants to do it, He will do it because He is in control. People say that all the time in the world and even in the church. However, it is an insult and an embarrassment to say God is in control of this world because it is a mess.

You can go to the drive-thru right now and order a meal, and you have a fifty-fifty chance that they even get it right. You are already on the road before you know they messed up. That is because it is a broken world. If God were in control, He would not mess up your order. Your food would not be cold; it would stay hot. You can apply this idea to everything down here.

Over the years at my job, I found discrepancies in my paycheck almost every month. A coworker figured it out and saw that the company had made mistakes in our paychecks for six years. I got back pay for six years of mistakes I did not know about, and it became a class-action lawsuit because someone else noticed it. God is not in control of that because He does not make mistakes. How can you pay your bills, and then have that company call you and say, "Hey, you need to pay your bills?" Now you have to prove you paid those bills by finding receipts. There are plenty of discrepancies, disappointments, and discouragements down here. However, God is not in control of those types of situations.

Now, God might be in control of your life because you invited Him in and included Him. However, God does not get involved if you do not go to the altar and dedicate your life and every part of your business, family, relationships, and everything about you. You must consciously and actively dedicate those things to God for Him to get involved, and this is the absolute truth.

GOD IS WAITING ON US— ## WE ARE NOT WAITING ON HIM

We think we are waiting on God down here, yet He is waiting on us. People think God is in control, and He is not because they have not asked Him into their lives. The world has chased God out of our schools and government and said they don't want Him there. Our schools and government all started to deteriorate at an alarming rate, then corruption and every evil came in. Suddenly we woke up, but it was almost too late because the manipulation and control were already there, and it would almost take a war to reverse the situation. God is not in control of this and is waiting on us. We are not waiting on Him.

When you get to Heaven, you will see that everything was established long ago. God revealed Himself and actively involved Himself; now He waits for us to respond to Him. We might be waiting on the Holy Spirit, but He has already been given, and God is waiting on us to invite Him in. The wake-up call comes when we get into overthrow. It is open season now, and we can do whatever we have in our hearts and spirit because that is where the Lord dwells and directs us. The demons do not know how to deal with a group of people like that. We are a serious threat to them.

The move of God has started. People are beginning to realize that God is waiting on them; He is not in control down here but wants to be in control through the church—through the believer. People are starting to realize that is their job. When people are accountable, knowing they will have to do something about it or it will not happen, this is when you get into overthrow. We see people praying, talking, and living that way more and more. These are leaders and history-makers who are no longer just surviving as victims. That is who you are, and it is all because of revelation, visitation, and habitation. You have been delivered, set free, and are now a leader.

You call the shots because God trusts you, just like He trusted Abraham, Moses, and David. They all did many exploits for God because God let them be who He made them to be.

11

THE KINGDOM OF GOD IS AT HAND

The time is fulfilled, and the kingdom of God is at hand.
Repent, and believe in the gospel.
—Mark 1:15

Jesus often talked about the kingdom of God. Interestingly, after He was raised from the dead, He was seen walking around the city, on the roads, and in many different places. Jesus appeared to many, and Acts 1:1–3 talks about how He taught about the kingdom of God for forty days after His resurrection. I am sure that the news of His crucifixion quickly spread around the city because He was so loved and hated by many people. You can imagine many people saw the crucifixion because Jesus was well-known and visible.

PREACHING THE GOSPEL OF THE
KINGDOM OF GOD

The former account I made, O Theophilus, of all that Jesus began both to do and teach, until the day in which He was taken up, after He through the Holy Spirit had given commandments to the apostles whom He had chosen, to whom He also presented Himself alive after His suffering by many infallible proofs, being seen by them during forty days and speaking of the things pertaining to the kingdom of God.

—Acts 1:1–3

If Jesus appeared to people for forty days after the crucifixion, how long do you think it took for that news to get around? The disciples and everyone must have been talking about it. Jesus chose to speak about and teach about the kingdom of God for forty days. The kingdom was the most important subject to Him and what the Father led Him to teach. Think about how Herod, Pilot, and all the Roman soldiers probably got wind of what happened. Who knows? Maybe some of them even saw Jesus. One of those centurion soldiers might have even seen Him talking to people during those forty days.

And this gospel of the kingdom will be preached in all the world as a witness to all the nations, and then the end will come.

—Matthew 24:14

Since Jesus said that the gospel of the kingdom must be preached in all the world, we need to think and be preaching it all the time. If Jesus picked this subject above all others to teach on for forty extra days after His death, burial, and resurrection, it should also be our priority. So what does that mean to us? And what does that have to do with holy fire and holiness? Once we have gone through this journey and yielded to the fire, we are ready to minister and preach to others. When we have allowed God to work with us and help us, we are prepared to release this message about the kingdom and Jesus.

REPENT AND BELIEVE IN THE GOSPEL

Jesus came to Galilee, preaching the gospel of the kingdom of God, and saying, "The time is fulfilled, and the kingdom of God is at hand. Repent, and believe in the gospel."

—Mark 1:14–15

Jesus came to Galilee and preached the gospel of the kingdom of God; this is what He said, and it is all recorded. I crave every word that comes from the mouth of God. Jesus said that people should not live by bread alone, but by every word that proceeds from the mouth of God (Matthew 4:4). I want to see everything I am supposed to see and hear everything I am supposed to hear. I desire to preach the kingdom and the gospel with accuracy and excellence.

I want to preach the gospel of God's kingdom according to the standard of Heaven. To do that, I must study and make myself available by the Spirit of God for the power of the resurrection to manifest. I will have to make myself available to be used in the gifts of the Spirit, prophetic utterances that God would need me to speak, and be ready to raise the dead and drive out demons. I will need to be prepared to do all this, as will you. However, what is crucial along with the kingdom's message is that we call people to repentance. We must share the gospel, announce the good news, and then call people to repentance. After they hear the good news, they have to turn to God; we have to bring people to that place of decision.

It is not enough to have a great message on Sunday in church or hear it on TV, YouTube, or whatever media you watch or read. That message has got to get you to a place where you turn, make a decision, and become accountable for what you just heard. We have discussed the message and its potency. We talked about how we must teach people about the fear of the Lord, brokenness, repentance, holy fire, holiness, sanctification, and all these different subjects. However, we must give people a chance to turn, repent, and acknowledge they fell short; then, we must provide them with the opportunity to make that decision to change. It is also good to do that publicly.

> *We need to not only preach the good news but also allow people to repent at the altar, turn to God, and get right with Him.*

We need to not only preach the good news but also allow people to repent at the altar, turn to God, and get right with Him. That is not happening today. Churches might have a great message, but it does not convince them to turn. And they are not given an opportunity to make a decision, which is most important. When Jesus presented His message, He taught repentance. If we are truly in Christ and genuinely moving by the Spirit, a point will come when the Holy Spirit, through us, allows people to make a decision and openly acknowledge it.

In Acts 17:28, Paul states that it is in Christ that we live, move, and have our being. This verse includes a resolution or a closure. Without a solution, I would not want to present a problem or dilemma to someone. Instead, when I share an issue, I want all parties involved able to walk away with a resolution. It is not enough to present a problem because people need closure. That closure is where people must be accountable and agree on a final resolution. That way, it never needs to be revisited once they walk away from it. They have agreed to a solution, which will happen. The involved parties trust each other to accomplish their part.

In the same way, the message of the kingdom of God must be presented with the opportunity for people to have a resolution. God has His desires, and then He makes them known. We hear them, but then we have to do something about it. Once we hear God's message, we must decide if we will believe it, agree with it, and abide by it. God gives His desires and tells us what He wants, and then He needs us to come into agreement with Him, which is a covenant. Through our accountability, we find closure. We know that if we meet all of God's desires and demands and He meets all of ours, He will seal this agreement. Then we can walk away knowing that it is all settled and resolved.

When you preach, share, and testify about Jesus, believe that God will confirm the word you preach with signs and wonders (Mark 16:20). When you do your part, God does His part. Jesus was doing what His Father wanted Him to do, but what the word was saying had to manifest. As a result of that preaching, people heard the word, mixed it with faith, and received it. Many people were delivered, healed, and raised from the dead. They were changed by what they heard and put their trust in Jesus. People must be given the same opportunity today.

THE KINGDOM OF GOD IS ADVANCING

Enter by the narrow gate; for wide is the gate and broad is the way that leads to destruction, and there are many who go in by it. Because narrow is the gate and difficult is the way which leads to life, and there are few who find it.

—Matthew 7:13–14

As we preach the kingdom of God, we must realize it is a real, literal place, a domain with a King ruling and reigning over it. God's kingdom realm has permeated this earthly realm through preaching and teaching the gospel and the demonstration of the power of the Spirit. As people receive the message of the kingdom, we have a harvest; they become subjects in the kingdom and part of the family of God because they hear the Word of God being preached. As the people grasp and take hold of that, the message must be preached about the holy fire, the advancing of the kingdom of God, and the entrance into that kingdom through the narrow way.

> *Let us be glad and rejoice and give Him glory, for the marriage of the Lamb has come, and His wife has made herself ready. And to her it was granted to be arrayed in fine linen, clean and bright, for the fine linen is the righteous acts of the saints. Then he said to me, "Write: 'Blessed are those who are called to the marriage supper of the Lamb!'" And he said to me, "These are the true sayings of God."*
>
> —Revelation 19:7–9

We enter the narrow way by separating ourselves from the world and subjecting ourselves to the Holy Spirit's work. As a result, we are disciplined and go through pruning, refinement by fire, and a cutting away as we are being purified. We are being readied for the marriage supper of the Lamb as the Lord's church, His body, His perfect bride without spot or wrinkle (Ephesians 5:26–27). The goal of the Holy Spirit is to get us ready so that we live and move in Him without any hindrance. The Holy Spirit is working and wants to present us perfect and above reproach to the Bridegroom, Jesus Christ. This is happening right now.

Not only will we get married to Jesus and sit at the marriage supper of the Lamb, but we will be given our next assignment. We are being readied for whatever we are promoted to by what we go through down here. You do not want to hide in your house, and you do not want to sit and wait for Jesus to come back; you want to make sure you are doing everything you can to be ready for the coming of the Lord. After that, everything that you encounter down here, all that you are being trained in, goes toward your next life, in the next job assignment that you will have.

PREPARING FOR ETERNITY

You are currently being readied for the job assignment you will be doing in eternity. You are an ambassador of Heaven and will represent God in other countries. Did you know there are other universes and not just our universe? God will put us in different places, and we will rule and reign with Him throughout eternity. It is so big, and we cannot comprehend it all now, but it is true anyway.

I want to give the Holy Spirit preeminence in my life right now, not just to prepare me for the marriage supper. It is beyond that. When

I was with Jesus, I was shown that I was being prepared for eternity as a representative of God and as someone in His household. I will be ministering for a long time, and so will you; we are all being made ready. You can be an example and an amazing minister down here, and it will continue forever. Be encouraged, and do not allow discouragement to come in because nothing is wasted at all. Everything you go through and learn will be used, and you will always remember how faithful God was to you down here.

INCREASING YOUR DISCERNMENT

You must allow to Lord to sharpen your discernment when you are going out and preaching the kingdom. You are part of the kingdom's expansion. Increasing your discernment is part of being a good warrior as you are being developed through holy fire. God wants you to have keen insight so you can see any situation, separate what is happening, and understand it.

Some people can look at something, like a camera or a table, and they can dissect it. They can see how it's built and discern situations you would not even begin to understand. Other people can look at a scenario or a problem and tell what is going on behind the scenes because they have the discernment to know how it functions. As born-again believers, we should be discerning in the Spirit and understand what is going on. We don't know everything, but it can be shown in the Spirit, whether good or evil. Our discernment in these last days needs to go to a higher level, and we need to know what God is saying and doing in situations.

At the end of the age, we will need to be wiser than ever. I see greater discernment coming to God's people. The holy fire will sharpen your discernment so that you will know right from wrong and be able to discern what is happening behind the scenes. You will even know what kind of spirits are operating, which happens with the gift of discerning of spirits, one of the gifts of the Spirit (1 Corinthians 12:1–11). However, we should all operate with simple discernment, which is a spiritual sensitivity to know what is happening around us.

BUILDING MOMENTUM

We also need to build momentum, which means you start to move in a specific direction and build up strength and power as you go. Think about how heavy a car is; it takes time to accelerate and gain momentum. But once you are traveling at a steady speed, you do not really notice the car's weight. The only time that you notice the car's weight is when you start and slow down. Braking and trying to slow down takes time because of the car's momentum and weight.

In the Spirit, momentum is when God sets you in a direction, and you start to build yourself up, becoming bold, strong, and established in what God has for you. You do not feel the weight once you get up to speed, but satan wants to slow you down and destroy that momentum. You are much weightier in the Spirit than you realize because you have accelerated and are either maintaining a certain speed or still accelerating. You can feel it when that is happening. Now, if someone wanted to slow you down, they would try to step in and distract you. If that happened, you could see and feel yourself decelerating.

You do not want satan to come in and hinder your momentum, which happens in different ways. One of the ways the devil does this is by drawing your attention away from God or creating situations so that you start to question Him. God is never working against you; He is accelerating and teaching you. Jesus wants to encourage you to discern between good and evil and everything that is going on around you in the spirit realm.

Jesus wants you to maintain momentum because a lot is invested in you. You have the Holy Spirit and the Word of God working inside you. You have the river of life and angels around you going back and forth from Heaven. You have ministry gifts inside you and the anointings of God upon you, and you have momentum. When you get groups of people together in agreement, even greater authority and momentum are established. The devil wants to slow down or destroy all this. Do not let anything get in your way to slow you down. Do not let it bother you when you face problems. Keep on going; continue thanking God and rejoicing. Do not let these evil spirits get in the way. The kingdom is full of discernment and momentum.

YOU HAVE BEEN GIVEN AUTHORITY

Assuredly, I say to you, whatever you bind on earth will be bound in Heaven, and whatever you loose on earth will be loosed in Heaven.

—Matthew 18:18

Another kingdom characteristic is that Jesus has a commanding air about Him. This idea of having a commanding air about you means that you are established in authority and sent like an ambassador. You have been given the authority to speak on behalf of someone in charge. You have been sent as a covenant keeper and representative of the kingdom. You represent the kingdom of God, and what you say goes. Jesus is giving you this ability.

√ I let the Word of God ignite in me. I allow that fire of the Holy Spirit to burn, and I feed the flame with the Word of God. Then I am ignited and speak from that place inside me; I speak from the fire. As Jesus has a commanding air about him, I want you to start to identify with Him and see He is the Commander. Yet that commanding air and authority have been given to you too. You must see yourself being ignited, meditating on the commands of the Lord in the Word of God. Then see that ignition happen so that you explode from within and walk with a commanding air about you.

I worked for an airline for many years, and I could tell a person of authority even when they were in plain clothes. When I checked on it, it was amazing because even though they did not have a uniform, I would find out they were high-ranking military, a police officer, or law enforcement. You could feel it because they had a commanding air about them, yet they did not have a visible badge or uniform. Despite dressing in street clothes, you could feel their authority, which is what I want for you. I want you to see that you are ignited with the Word of God and the fire of God and that you have a commanding air about you.

12

A STANDARD FOR OUR GENERATION

So shall My word be that goes forth from My mouth; It
shall not return to Me void, but it shall accomplish
what I please, and it shall prosper in the thing
for which I sent it.
—Isaiah 55:11

I often start to see and think about where God is. I picture what happened when Isaiah saw the Lord high and lifted up and saw all the activities taking place in the throne room. He was undone. I often think about how incredible it was for a human body to be taken to see the Lord and witness how majestic and full of authority He is. I think of what it is like to see the white-hot fire in the throne room, all the living creatures there, and the holiness that fills it. The experience was so amazing and powerful that Isaiah says he was undone.

> *In the year that King Uzziah died, I saw the Lord sitting on a throne, high and lifted up, and the train of His robe filled the temple. Above it stood seraphim; each one had six wings: with two he covered his face, with two he covered his feet, and with two he flew. And one cried to another and said: "Holy, holy, holy is the Lord of hosts; The whole earth is full of His glory!" And the posts of the door were shaken by the voice of him who cried out, and the house was filled with smoke. So I said: "Woe is me, for I am undone! Because I am a man of unclean lips, And I dwell in the midst of a people of unclean lips; For my eyes have seen the King, the Lord of hosts."*

—Isaiah 6:1–5

GOD IS IN COMMAND AND HAS FULL AUTHORITY

As we discussed, the Lord wants us to walk in an air of command, having full authority. God wants us to remember where He sits and that He is the great I Am in Heaven, the Creator of everything. We do not see Him in control, ruling and reigning here on earth, but He certainly rules and reigns in Heaven in full authority. God is in control of Heaven, and He deals with this earthly realm through us, the church, through the believers. We need to be good ambassadors and be on fire from the fire at the altar of the throne of God. The seraphim there are on fire, and we can see the full authority, the beauty, and the fear of the Lord. The holiness of the Lord is so evident there with a crisp holy presence where God is in command.

Everything God says is essential, and our response to Him should be one of awe. God speaks from His throne, giving out the commands for what He wants to accomplish. Everything God says goes forth and does not return empty because it accomplishes what He intends. We can think about how powerful God is, yet even though He is the King of the kingdom and His domain, He is also our Father, and we are His children. We are so privileged to be part of His family. We have free access to the Father, not just as servants, slaves, or subjects of the kingdom but as children of a loving Heavenly Father. We can approach and encounter God with a child's heart. We have free access to the throne without even being invited.

The Spirit Himself bears witness with our spirit that
we are children of God, and if children, then heirs—

*heirs of God and joint heirs with Christ, if indeed we
suffer with Him, that we may also be glorified
together.*

—Romans 8:16–17

Part of what we do and preach in the kingdom down here is that we
must remember where our authority is: in the throne room, where
the fire from the throne is, especially since we have a Heavenly
Father who loves us. The Father has made us part of his family—
we are heirs of God and co-heirs with Jesus. So we need to hear
what our Father is speaking and then repeat it. We need to operate
in that authority from the throne and speak what He says.

YOUR HOME IS IN HEAVEN

*The Lord is not slack concerning His promise, as
some count slackness, but is longsuffering toward us,
not willing that any should perish but that all should
come to repentance.*

—2 Peter 3:9

Remember that God loves people and does not want anyone to
perish; He desires that everyone has everlasting life. We love people
because God loves people. We are part of His family and want other
people to become part of that family as well. The kingdom of God

is expanding and not just as a king with people under him but as a Heavenly Father that loves us and loves people; He wants them to come in and inherit this kingdom. Always remember that this is your origin and where you belong. You will return there one day and discover Heaven was always your home.

When I was there with Jesus, I was home and realized that anything I do for Him is out of my love for Him. I am just here visiting and am not part of this world system. When you are in the throne room where you belong, you understand that Heaven clearly was and is your home. Everything about Heaven is who you are. Down here on earth, you will feel uncomfortable. You will not feel accepted or fit in, which is common for all believers.

You must remind yourself that you are just visiting down here and are actually living your life out of love for God. That makes it a little easier to deal with life down here. I always longed to go back there and be part of what God is doing in Heaven because that is where my heart is, and it never leaves there. That is the way it is with you too. I have free access to go there in the Spirit at all times, but I also know Heaven will be my permanent dwelling place someday.

LEARN TO FEED YOURSELF THE WORD OF GOD

As a minister of the kingdom, you will be ministering the Word of God, and while you are down here, you will have to feed yourself in the Spirit. You will find that as you grow in the Lord and are filled with the holy fire, you are way beyond what you encounter around you. You will get to where you will find that only certain people or organizations feed you, and you will often have to feed yourself. That is why I allow myself time to study the Word of God daily and meditate on it, knowing that it might be the only hot meal I get for the day or the week. You must learn to feed yourself a hot meal in the Spirit because you might not get it from someone else.

As you submit yourself to the holy fire, your standard is of the highest level, and the holy fire will reveal all the things that need to go. Once you allow that to happen, you will only want the highest level and might not find that everywhere. If you are going to be a minister of the kingdom, you will have to learn to feed yourself with fiery messages that you receive yourself from the Word of God. I prepare meals for myself by studying the Word of God, meditating, and praying. I attach myself to the Word of God.

I want and need to hear from my Heavenly Father, so I attach myself to His words and latch myself onto the truth. I then pray in the Spirit often, which is my lifeline. Besides feeding myself a hot meal, I latch myself onto the Father and whatever He might say to me. Then I also pray in the Spirit as much as possible because that is the breath that keeps me going. I literally feel like I am attached to the Father, and He is the only One that keeps me going.

At some points in life, you might have no one else to help you as God Himself can. We still need the body of Christ; however, you must learn to feed yourself, attach yourself to your Father, and pray in the Spirit as though it is the very breath you need.

PRAYING IN TONGUES WITH THE UNDERSTANDING

Therefore let him who speaks in a tongue pray that he may interpret. For if I pray in a tongue, my spirit prays, but my understanding is unfruitful.
—1 Corinthians 14:13-14

I wish you all spoke with tongues, but even more that you prophesied; for he who prophesies is greater than he who speaks with tongues, unless indeed he interprets, that the church may receive edification.
—1 Corinthians 14:5

I speak in tongues a great deal and pray in the Spirit as much as possible. I pray silently in public and do it out loud in private. Then I pray that God would help me interpret or understand what is being said, even if it is just a word or two or a little glimpse of understanding. It is vital to gain some understanding because the Holy Spirit wants to take you in a direction, and your mind is not always fruitful. Sometimes, signposts along the way will let you know what is happening.

Paul said that we should pray that we can interpret, so I encourage you to pray that the Lord allows you to interpret your tongues and gain some understanding. He said, if you prophesy, you understand what you are saying because it is in your own language. I want to encourage you with that as well.

MOVING WHEN GOD MOVES

Then Jesus said to His disciples, "If anyone desires to come after Me, let him deny himself, and take up his cross, and follow Me."

—Matthew 16:24

At times, you will have to deny yourself and your flesh. Temptations come up, and you will have to say no to your flesh and mind, which is part of how the kingdom operates. At times, God will have priorities and will want you to do some things for Him that may involve changing your schedule and your own plans. If you really want to move with God in the kingdom and accomplish His heart's desire, you must be willing to move when He moves.

> *If you really want to move with God in the kingdom and accomplish His heart's desire, you must be willing to move when He moves.*

At times, I am sure Jesus wanted to rest and sleep, yet He was often interrupted. I don't know how much He even slept in His three-and-a-half years on earth. Many supernatural miracles happened during the day, but He would go into the mountains at night to pray. You might find yourself not sleeping at times because you have to pray, and then, during the day, you are ministering. Sometimes you will have to let your schedule be interrupted to fulfill what God has for you, which is also denying yourself.

Denying yourself is not just about trying to overcome temptation and sin. A time comes when you rest and walk with God. But God may also move you in a direction so that you deny yourself more than seems possible. Everyone deserves to rest, sleep, and have time for themselves. However, the Lord may have you do some things at times that are very important to Him, which is all part of life in the kingdom, walking in the supernatural, and denying yourself.

You must keep your edge about you in the Spirit, which is not easy. Even though you may think it's easy, you struggle because this is a fallen world. You can fall into chaos if you do not maintain your fire for the Lord. Notice that possessions break and don't fix themselves. They get dirty and don't clean themselves. They don't put themselves together. We see our stuff go from order to chaos all the time because of this fallen world, and it deteriorates and falls apart. You must maintain your walk with the Lord as you do with your natural possessions.

YOU ARE REWARDED FOR EVERYTHING YOU DO FOR GOD

But without faith it is impossible to please Him, for he who comes to God must believe that He is, and that He is a rewarder of those who diligently seek Him.

—Hebrews 11:6

Hebrews says it is impossible to please God without faith, so you must have faith. It continues by saying that he who comes to God must believe He is. That is easy because you know that God exists.

It's harder to believe that God is a rewarder of those who diligently seek Him because you have to get rid of that rejection mentality that tells you that God won't reward you. Yet you will get a reward for everything you do for God. Recording angels are constantly taking notes and reporting on you, writing a book of remembrance.

> *Then those who feared the Lord spoke to one another, and the Lord listened and heard them; So a book of remembrance was written before Him for those who fear the Lord and who meditate on His name. "They shall be Mine," says the Lord of hosts, "On the day that I make them My jewels. And I will spare them as a man spares his own son who serves him." Then you shall again discern between the righteous and the wicked, between one who serves God and one who does not serve Him.*
>
> —Malachi 3:16–18

This verse in Malachi shows that books of remembrance are written for those who do right and honor the Lord. You have to believe that God exists, but you also have to believe that He is a rewarder of those who *diligently* seek Him. You have got to seek God, and the word there is *diligently*, which means you throw everything else aside and count the cost. The parable of the pearl of great price essentially instructs us to just go for it, giving all that we have in exchange for all He has for us (Matthew 13:45–46).

DILIGENTLY SEEKING GOD IN FAITH

*As the deer pants for the water brooks, so pants my
soul for You, O God.*

—Psalm 42:1

I always pray, "Lord, make me willing to be willing. I give You permission to overcome my will. Overcome me, Lord, overwhelm me, convince me, win me over, work on me. I permit you to work me over." I have prayed that prayer for forty years since I was first saved. I want to know Him, and I must be convinced that He rewards me because I am diligently, aggressively, and outwardly seeking Him.

Diligently seeking God is not a religious exercise or mental agreement but a heartfelt drawing toward God. I desire Him, just like David expressed in Psalm 42:1. Like a thirsty deer desires water, this is how we should be with God. That was how David was—he was a seeker of God. I want to be like a child and discover the Lord as a treasure. I want to seek God and find Him. I want to find that treasure, the mysteries of God; I long to know the deep secrets of the kingdom. Now is the time to seek the Lord and get oil in your lamps. It is time to discover what God is doing and saying in the Spirit.

In the world right now, we have a lot of rebellious, strong-willed people that are opinionated and violent. We have all kinds of corruption at the highest levels. We have stealing, fraud, and evil happening around us. Yet with all that around us, we can diligently seek God, and He will take us into the land of Goshen, just like in Egypt. The Israelites were in Goshen and did not encounter all the plagues in Egypt (Exodus 9:13–35).

What pleases God? It is when we seek Him diligently and have faith. Faith pleases God, and He rewards us (Hebrews 11:6). Part of faith is diligently seeking Him so I will see the fruit of my labor. I will see that my diligence pays off. I have committed to building my faith, staying there, submitting myself to the holy fire, and seeing a whole generation change. I will see a deluge of God's power in this day we live and see people's lives change. We will see the harvest come in and see people set free, it will be the longest and greatest move of God we have ever seen. It will be a continual move that will usher Jesus into this generation. We can see that happen.

Sadly, we must have another move of God because we have slowed down our momentum and cooled off our fire for the Lord, making that move necessary. As warriors, as students of the Word of God, we must yield and let God use us to bring this move upon the earth. However, you will have to be really hot, very persistent, and fully convinced because it will be an aggressive move with the power of God. People in certain denominations will criticize it because they are not part of it. The move of God is happening outside denominations that did not want to be part of it.

For example, when you vote God out of schools and the government, suddenly, they are left to themselves, and then the system becomes corrupt. That is why we have the corruption that we have now. That is why people think they have to steal to win. They believe they must take from people because they cannot just get it honestly. That is what the enemy is doing all the time: stealing, killing, and destroying, but Jesus is blessing people because Jesus gives us life (John 10:10). He wants to teach us how to live, receiving from Heaven and giving life out—that interaction from the realm of Heaven to earth.

Certain people in history that I studied were rejected by the established religion of their day, yet they were heroes of faith. They are celebrated now but were not accepted when they were alive. It is interesting how that has happened throughout history. Jesus addressed the Pharisees, saying He had sent them many prophets, but they killed them all. Later, they celebrated those same prophets as their heroes (Matthew 23:29–37). Then He told them that they would do the same to Him: They would kill Him.

All the people we celebrate in history were not liked when they were alive. At the time, they were needed, but they were not popular. Think about some of the things people have stood up for and how we are free now because of it. Think about how women were not allowed to vote. It was ridiculous that they were considered less than others and could not vote, but the government still taxed them for working.

We go through all these struggles; some seem so ridiculous that it's hard to believe they were ever an issue. However, people had to stand up for women's rights and against racism at that time. Today we think, *How did we even have to struggle with that? It is all about revelation.* People God used in their generation had to stand up for the standard God put inside them. It was difficult then, but now we enjoy those freedoms because of the stand they took. In the same way, Jesus paid the price for us; now, we are all called to bear a standard for our generation.

13

KEEP MOVING INTO THE FIRE

Rejoice and be exceedingly glad, for great is your reward in Heaven, for so they persecuted the prophets who were before you.

—Matthew 5:12

All of us know people who go from church to church and even from denomination to denomination. Some of these people are simply church hopping. But others are looking for strong movements of God. These holy-fire, Holy Spirit–led groups of people at some point became denominations and were very popular and very large in their day. If I named them, you would know who they were and are today. Why do people leave one denomination for another? Well, when God was moving, they loved the church and were deeply involved. But the leaders of the denominations eventually stopped the move of God, so people left and looked for another church where God kept moving.

People want to keep moving with God. If a denomination stops moving, they will leave and go where the fire is. As we have been discussing, we must stay diligent and on fire in our humanness and this fallen world.

DON'T LET YOUR MOMENTUM SLIP FROM YOU

It is imperative that we keep moving and be more sober-minded and aggressive because these truths can slip from us. As I said, order goes to chaos; chaos does not go to order. In other words, your house, car, room, and bedroom do not clean or fix themselves. Our possessions break, get dirty, and get out of order, but you never see it in reverse. Your car doesn't fix itself, your bed doesn't make itself, and your house doesn't clean itself.

This broken world goes from order to chaos. You can make your bed and clean your house, but you will have to do it again in a couple of weeks. You might not be able to explain why that happens, but it does, and that is how it is. You must always be diligent, stay on fire, and keep reminding yourself that you are led by the Spirit and not by the flesh.

EVIL SPIRITS TRAP PEOPLE IN BONDAGE WITH FEAR AND CONTROL

As you discover the history of a denomination, you may think, *Oh, I want to be a part of this.* After being part of that denomination for a while, you might notice the leaders are controlling and manipulative. The same thing can happen with relationships. At first, everything seems great, and suddenly, instead of letting you make decisions and being free to be you, you start to feel controlled and manipulated. That is also what happens with big government.

In essence, you hire the government. You pay your taxes so they can protect and serve you. The government is supposed to take care of what you don't have time to do, and you pay taxes for them to do that. Suddenly, the government is telling you what you should believe and what you can and cannot do, which is manipulation and control. It eventually becomes a dictatorship, which is the antichrist spirit in operation.

> *And you He made alive, who were dead in trespasses*
> *and sins, in which you once walked according to the*

course of this world, according to the prince of the
power of the air, the spirit who now works in the sons
of disobedience, among whom also we all once
conducted ourselves in the lusts of our flesh,
fulfilling the desires of the flesh and of the mind, and
were by nature children of wrath, just as the others.

—Ephesians 2:1–3

When religion and relationships become manipulative, the powers of the spirit of the air, which are under lucifer (satan), are in operation. These evil spirits entrap people in bondage through control and fear. If you do not allow the Holy Spirit to keep you free and moving, you may get into a group where you find yourself being controlled. Instead of walking in freedom, you will learn how to manipulate and control people. Operating in that wicked spirit is wrong, but it is part of religion.

For they bind heavy burdens, hard to bear, and lay
them on men's shoulders; but they themselves will
not move them with one of their fingers.

—Matthew 23:4

In Matthew 23:4, Jesus rebuked the Pharisees because they manipulated and controlled the people, putting heavy yokes on them. Jesus told the Pharisees they were supposed to take the heavy burdens off people instead of enslaving them. Jesus came to remove the yokes. Be aware of this deception happening in the world today. Jesus hates religion, corrupt government, and control.

IF YOU LOVE GOD, KEEP HIS COMMANDMENTS

> *If you love Me, keep My commandments.*
>
> —John 14:15

God, Who has given us free will, invites us to come to Him. However, God tells us what He likes and lets us know that if we want to know and serve Him, we must do what He commands as John 14:15 says. If we say we want God yet don't do what He commands, we cannot expect His benefits.

> *If you abide in Me, and My words abide in you, you will ask what you desire, and it shall be done for you.*
>
> —John 15:7

People say they prayed but did not get what they prayed for. Well, is His Word abiding in you, and are you abiding in Him? I often find Christians are putting stipulations on God, and they are not in a position to do that, but they do not seem to know it. They say, "I don't believe in healing because I'm not healed." Or "I don't believe in prosperity because I'm broke." The real problem is that they do not want to come under the authority of the Lord and abide in Him. They only want the benefits of knowing Him. Jesus hates that attitude because He wants to build up people, and He wants people to come to Him willingly.

DO NOT GIVE OUT OF COMPULSION OR MANIPULATION

But this I say: He who sows sparingly will also reap sparingly, and he who sows bountifully will also reap bountifully. So let each one give as he purposes in his heart, not grudgingly or of necessity; for God loves a cheerful giver. And God is able to make all grace abound toward you, that you, always having all sufficiency in all things, may have an abundance for every good work.

—2 Corinthians 9:6–8

Paul said, "God loves a cheerful giver." You should not give out of compulsion or for your own benefit. When you give, God can bless you, and you can have abundance not only for your own needs but then have extra to give to others. The whole idea here is that you should not give out of compulsion. You should not give because people manipulate your emotions and tell you how much they need the money. Paul told the Corinthians that he wanted them to take the offering before he even came to speak to them. He did not want them to feel compelled, manipulated, or pressured into giving (1 Corinthians 16:1–2).

We should give because we love God, and He loves a cheerful giver. In other words, I give to God because I love Him, which is part of my worship. When you give of your finances, it is in response to God's goodness; you love Him and want to give, not out of compulsion. When you give, you sow into God and reap the benefits of sowing into Him. When you partner with people, you love what God is doing and want to be part of that. So you should never do anything out of compulsion because Jesus hates manipulation and control.

> *Exposing yourself to the holy fire, being humble, and staying hot prevent you from succumbing to the spirit of the world.*

Our enemy, satan, is a dictator and a terrorist. He makes people afraid and enslaves them. He raises nations, governments, and dictators that manipulate and victimize their people with too much power. They are supposed to be serving their people and not controlling them. In this day that we live in, we must be careful that the spirit of the world does not get into the church. Exposing yourself to the holy fire, being humble, and staying hot prevent you from succumbing to the spirit of the world. Even though you are fighting this law of going from order to chaos and its pull on you, you can walk free of that pull. However, even though that pull does not affect you, you must always be mindful.

TAKE TIME TO EXAMINE YOURSELF

We should take communion because we must take time to examine ourselves and remember what Jesus did for us. I am finding that people who have problems with sin consciousness and do not feel forgiven have a deeply rooted mindset. We must remind ourselves what Jesus did for us by taking communion. We are connected and accountable to the body of Christ and everyone around us, because if one hurts, the body hurts.

> *Therefore whoever eats this bread or drinks this cup of the Lord in an unworthy manner will be guilty of the body and blood of the Lord. But let a man examine himself, and so let him eat of the bread and*

drink of the cup. For he who eats and drinks in an unworthy manner eats and drinks judgment to himself, not discerning the Lord's body. For this reason many are weak and sick among you, and many sleep. For if we would judge ourselves, we would not be judged. But when we are judged, we are chastened by the Lord, that we may not be condemned with the world.

—1 Corinthians 11:27–32

> *I would like you to take communion and think about what the Lord has done for you. Consider your responsibility to the body.*

In these verses, I want to emphasize that we need to discern the body of the Lord and know what the Lord did for us with His blood and body. We must understand that we are forgiven and that we forgive others. We also do not want to shorten our lives by not discerning the Lord's body. Paul said that many people who don't discern fall asleep, which refers to people who die early. Falling asleep is about death; we do not want to shorten our lives.

We do not want to miss out on what God has for us. We do not want to be lukewarm, fall asleep, and die early, so we must discern what Jesus has done for us. I would like you to take communion and think about what the Lord has done for you. Consider your responsibility to the body. Falling asleep early is not about taking a nap; it is literally premature death because a person failed to discern the body and the blood of Jesus. When you sit at the table and take communion, you must discern what that means and take it as a holy and sacred act. You set yourself apart for the Lord.

> *It is actually reported that there is sexual immorality among you, and such sexual immorality as is not even named among the Gentiles—that a man has his father's wife! And you are puffed up, and have not rather mourned, that he who has done this deed might be taken away from among you. For I indeed, as absent in body but present in spirit, have already judged (as though I were present) him who has so done this deed. In the name of our Lord Jesus Christ, when you are gathered together, along with my spirit, with the power of our Lord Jesus Christ, deliver such a one to satan for the destruction of the flesh, that his spirit may be saved in the day of the Lord Jesus. Your glorying is not good. Do you not know that a little leaven leavens the whole lump?*

196

Therefore purge out the old leaven, that you may be a new lump, since you truly are unleavened. For indeed Christ, our Passover, was sacrificed for us.

—1 Corinthians 5:1–7

In these verses in this letter, Paul addresses the sexual immorality in the Corinthian church. He told them that such abominations were going on there that he had not even heard of in the world. Paul said to them that when they were gathered together and the Spirit of the Lord was there, his spirit would be there also; they were to turn that sexually immoral person over to satan. Paul was not physically there, but he said even though he was absent in the body, he was present in the spirit. He said when they gathered together, the presence and power of God were there with them.

GOD'S JUDGMENT IN THE LAST DAYS

In 1 Corinthians 5:1–7, Paul described being absent in the body but present in the spirit, which is a step beyond most people's understanding; it has to do with apostolic authority. These types of judgments will happen again in these last days. We will also see situations like what happened with Ananias and Sapphira, who were slain for lying to the Holy Spirit (Acts 5:1–11). Paul instructed the Corinthian church to deliver the man practicing sexual sin to satan for the destruction of the flesh, that his spirit may be saved in the day of the Lord Jesus.

Paul wanted to set an example for the whole church so that they would not permit wickedness. If Paul let this situation continue without addressing it and let that person have his father's wife, it would condone those kinds of behaviors in Corinth. So Paul needed to set that example. He claimed he would be there with them in spirit, even though he was not there in the body, and this is amazing. When it comes to outward sin that the world and the church see, discipline must be established so that it does not spread into other areas.

After they put that man out, he was not allowed to return to the church and fellowship with them because he chose to sin and be part of the world. He was sent out, and because of that, we have this record, and that man repented in the end. He felt sorrowful and decided that what he did was not worth losing out on the Lord and fellowship. As the man repented and was grieving, Paul, in his second letter, told the Corinthians that it had been enough.

Paul instructed the Corinthians to bring the man who had been with his father's wife back after he repented so satan would not win him over with overwhelming grief (2 Corinthians 2:6–11). The destruction of that man's flesh so that his soul might be saved was accelerated so that it fixed the problem. Paul told them they should bring that man back into fellowship so that satan did not outfox them. This account has to do with apostolic authority, but it also has to do with the fact that the world and people in the church are watching, so we need to enforce holiness and correct behavior. It is okay to make decisions about the behavior of brothers and sisters in the body.

> *Arise, shine; for your light has come! And the glory of the Lord is risen upon you. For behold, the darkness shall cover the earth, and deep darkness the people; but the Lord will arise over you, and His glory will be seen upon you. The Gentiles shall come to your light, and kings to the brightness of your rising.*
>
> —Isaiah 60:1–3

In the last days, with the intensity of the Spirit of God coming upon the earth, the move of God, and the harvest, we will see more manifestations than ever before. In his vision, Daniel saw that people moving in the Spirit were wise and bright with their faces shining; Isaiah saw this as well (Daniel 12:1–4; Isaiah 9:2). In the last days, we will also see apostolic authority dealing with sin, like with Paul in Corinth. We could see God's judgment manifest as it did with Ananias and Sapphira. Jude 1:14–15 mentions Enoch's prophecy concerning the coming judgment against wickedness.

DEMONS FEEL THE HEAT OF THE
HOLY FIRE IN YOU

Those who are wise shall shine like the brightness of the firmament, and those who turn many to righteousness like the stars forever and ever.

—Daniel 12:3

God's people will be the bright and shining ones in the last days. The intensity of the Spirit will reach the point where we will see instant judgment or things happening immediately that would not normally occur. When you start moving in the Spirit, you become hotter and hotter and start moving into the spiritual realm. The demons around you or people you are affiliated with this whole time are fine until you start moving into that realm. Suddenly, those demons will feel the heat turned up and start acting up; you may wonder what is happening. The temperature in you will be raised to the point where the demons will be uncomfortable, whereas before, they were not bothered.

When the move of the Holy Spirit intensifies in churches, the demons start acting up because people are getting hot. At that point, the people that do not want to go on with God begin having issues with the move of God, and they complain. Then satan will use some of those people, especially those who have a lot of money and can influence the church, to pressure the pastor and discourage the people who are on fire. We are legitimately supposed to be operating at that level with the holy fire, but unfortunately, the people that don't want that might influence the pastor. I want you to be ready in case this happens.

God may give you a dream or a visitation, He might have you praying in tongues more, or He might have you missing meals. However, I promise that once you start fasting, praying, and pursuing the Lord and holy fire, the demons will suddenly feel uncomfortable. When you enter the fire, you get hotter, and wherever you go, what used to be okay is not okay anymore. Problems will start to stir up, and people will shift and change, and then you will see that those demons were there the whole time, but they were not bothered like they are now.

As you start moving in the kingdom, preaching the kingdom, getting hotter, and not putting up with lukewarmness, the demons entrenched in the people around you will begin to act up; you must be ready for this. You will have dreams, visions, and experiences with the Lord that will bring you higher, but those around you who do not go up with you will have a problem. People will act up, scream, and say things they shouldn't. You will face resistance, manipulation, and control. You may think, *If I had not prayed or fasted as much and had just stayed the same, everyone would still like me as they did back then.* The problem is they liked you back then because you were not making a difference.

> *Rejoice and be exceedingly glad, for great is your reward in Heaven, for so they persecuted the prophets who were before you.*
>
> —Matthew 5:12

If you want to make a difference, you will inherit what Jesus inherited. Everywhere Jesus went, He was doing the Father's will, and devils were being driven out. The Pharisees flipped out because they had controlling spirits and did not like Jesus. I want to prepare you so that you will be ready for this kind of resistance when you face it. When it does happen, remember what Jesus said in Matthew 5:12. You will be rewarded in Heaven for your stand, but you will be persecuted down here for it.

14

SAVED, HEALED, AND DELIVERED

And this gospel of the kingdom will be preached in all
the world as a witness to all the nations,
and then the end will come.
—Matthew 24:14

The move of God has already started, and the Lord will bring in a future harvest of people. You have to realize that God wants to populate Heaven; however, we have to pray for this to happen and participate in it. A time is coming when people will be healed every time they get together with believers. When people are brought in to hear the gospel, there will be healings, deliverances, and manifestations of the gifts of the Spirit (1 Corinthians 12:7–11). There will be words of knowledge, words of wisdom, and all kinds of miracles. People will be full of joy, laughing, and having breakthroughs. All their yokes will be broken off, and their heavy burdens and bondages will leave.

THE HOLY FIRE IS GETTING YOU READY FOR THE MOVE OF GOD

Expect the angels to bring people to you. They will bring the unsaved in to be saved, the sick to be healed, and the demon-possessed to be delivered. God wants to give words to you by the Holy Spirit so that you can minister to people with words of knowledge and words of wisdom. I want you to be ready for this move of God, and the holy fire is preparing you for that.

We must submit to this fire. When the angels come, they ignite you with fire because they are flames of fire. The Spirit of the Lord is always willing; He brings freedom wherever He is welcome. Be expecting miracles of healing and deliverance, and they will come. I meditate on all this and anticipate how this move of God is coming.

For as many as are led by the Spirit of God, these are sons of God. For you did not receive the spirit of bondage again to fear, but you received the Spirit of adoption by whom we cry out, "Abba, Father."

—Romans 8:14–15

Romans 8:14–15 is an important verse to understand. The Spirit of adoption is the Spirit of full acceptance, and the Holy Spirit confirms that acceptance, crying out, "Abba, Father." He calls out "Father, Father," because we are His children, accepted and written into the will of God. We are heirs of God and co-heirs with Jesus (Romans 8:17).

And I will ask the Father, and He will give you another Helper (Comforter, Advocate, Intercessor— Counselor, Strengthener, Standby), to be with you forever—the Spirit of Truth, whom the world cannot receive [and take to its heart] because it does not see Him or know Him, but you know Him because He (the Holy Spirit) remains with you continually and will be in you. "I will not leave you as orphans [comfortless, bereaved, and helpless]; I will come [back] to you. After a little while the world will no longer see Me, but you will see Me; because I live, you will live also. On that day [when that time

comes] you will know for yourselves that I am in My
Father, and you are in Me, and I am in you."

—John 14:16–20 AMP

In this passage, Jesus describes the Holy Spirit as an enforcer of the blessing and a very aggressive advocate or lawyer. Jesus gives us all these names or different characteristics of the Holy Spirit in the Amplified Version—Helper, Comforter, Advocate, Intercessor, Counselor, Strengthener, Standby, and Spirit of Truth; He enforces the covenant and the blessing. He will not only present you blameless to the Lord on that day, but He is perfecting you now in preparation for the move of God and the harvest of souls (Jude 1:24). Then you will be ready for your job in the next life to come as well.

MANY WILL NOT TOLERATE SOUND DOCTRINE AND WILL TURN AWAY FROM THE TRUTH

For the time will come when they will not endure
sound doctrine, but according to their own desires,
because they have itching ears, they will heap up for
themselves teachers; and they will turn their ears
away from the truth, and be turned aside to fables.

—2 Timothy 4:3–4

In these last days, controversy will arise concerning doctrine and people's behavior, which is already happening and will continue to increase. People will turn away from the truth and turn to fables, so the Lord wants us to be ready for that. We will preach the pure gospel, the pure message of the kingdom, and then the end will come (Matthew 24:14). The Lord tells us to preach an aggressive message, this gospel of deliverance, healing, and debt cancellation. God confirms this message with signs and wonders, such as setting people free and raising the dead. He is a good God, who is not hurting people or causing problems, but that does not go over well with religious folks.

Often, religious people think God is making them sick and poor, causing all the trouble and destruction we see. These people just give up and say, "Well, you know, that must be what God wants." They do not know the Bible because God clearly says He is a good God, and it is the thief who hurts people. Jesus came to give us life and life more abundantly (John 10:10).

OUR GOD IS GOOD

Jesus said to him, "Have I been with you so long, and yet you have not known Me, Philip? He who has seen Me has seen the Father; so how can you say, 'Show us the Father?'"

—John 14:9

I trust in Jesus because He was the express image of the Father, sent to be our example (Hebrews 1:3). I will believe in God's blessings, which the Holy Spirit continuously enforces. The Holy Spirit reminds us of what Jesus said and will show us the future (John 14:26; 16:13). We must tell people that God is a good God (Jeremiah 29:11).

When Jesus appeared to me, He told me about the testing coming upon the church and the earth. He gave this warning because we were lukewarm. He explained that satan—not He and His Father—was causing these calamities. It is very interesting how religious people will side with the devil as to what is happening on the earth and think it's God. They say things like, "We're getting what we deserve." I am shocked at the religious people's responses and mentalities, but we were warned about them. As Paul said, the time will come when they will not tolerate sound doctrine.

The Lord wants to bless people in these last days with good health. He wants to bless them with freedom in their minds and to set them free from demonic spirits (Luke 4:18–19). God wants people to be financially blessed and prosperous in everything they do so that all their needs are met; then, they will have extra to help others. This is God's desire and what He is speaking to everyone. To share the message of the gospel is to preach jubilee, which was debt cancellation; to break bondages, not put them on; to heal the sick, not put sickness onto them; to deliver people from the demonic; and to raise the dead.

When the gospel is demonstrated, people are not dying; they are being raised from the dead. They are being healed and delivered, they are prospering, their sins are forgiven, and they are full of joy. Jesus preached the gospel, expressing how much His Father loves you. You can go to the Father on your own, using Jesus's name (John 16:23–28). Jesus said that if you love, embrace, and obey His Father, They will come to live with you (John 14:20–23). Jesus said that you could ask whatever you desire—not what you need, but what you desire—and it shall be done for you (John 15:7–11). He said this would be done to give glory to the Father and that your joy may be complete (John 16:24). That is in the Scripture. I do not see any scholar trying to discredit or fight over this passage.

THE UNFORGIVABLE SIN

Yet some people do not believe that God is a good God and that He answers every prayer. As Paul said to Timothy, people in the last days will not put up with sound doctrine. The holy fire and the move of God are increasing; the spiritual temperature is rising. In these times of lukewarmness, when people are falling away, it is dangerous to attribute the works of the devil to God. It is also very dangerous to say that the devil is working when it is God, for example, to say that speaking in tongues is of the devil. If you attribute the works of the Holy Spirit to the works of the devil, according to what Jesus said, that is not forgivable (Mark 3:28–29).

> *Therefore I say to you, every sin and blasphemy will be forgiven men, but the blasphemy against the Spirit will not be forgiven men. Anyone who speaks a word against the Son of Man, it will be forgiven him; but whoever speaks against the Holy Spirit, it will not be forgiven him, either in this age or in the age to come.*
> —Matthew 12:31–32

If you speak against the Spirit of God, Jesus said it is not forgivable in this life or the next. He said you could speak against the Father and the Son, but you cannot speak against the Holy Spirit. I do not understand everything that entails, but I am smart enough to know not to do that. In these last days, when I listen to people mock Christians that believe in the Holy Spirit, miracles, and speaking in tongues, I cringe; it is unpardonable to attribute that to the enemy. Jesus said that is unforgivable.

ALLOW THE FIRE OF GOD TO CONSUME YOU

In the future, people will oppose the work of God and His move. They are on dangerous ground when they come against healing, deliverance, debt cancellation, speaking in tongues, and walking in the Spirit—as mentioned, this is unforgivable. The last days are upon us, and if we are going to serve the Lord and go the whole way with Him, we need to be hot and allow the fire to consume us. If we don't, people could fall away very quickly. You must either be hot or cold; lukewarm people won't last because of the spiritual environment that we are in.

> *Share all the good things the gospel brings: healing, the forgiveness of sin, debt cancellation, and God's supernatural financial provision.*

I call all the people associated with me to turn and repent and get hot. Allow the Word of God to ignite within you and give the Spirit of God free rein. Talk all the time about how good God is; speak about deliverance and freedom. Share all the good things the gospel brings: healing, the forgiveness of sin, debt cancellation, and God's supernatural financial provision. Discuss the ministry of angels. As you do this, you build each other up in faith, and then the kingdom of God advances. If people in the world don't want to hear about the kingdom, we can still encourage each other. We can always call friends, build them up, and preach to them. I am sure you can find someone who would want to listen to your preaching.

In these last days, give your finances to the Lord. With holy fire, God needs to know that you can be trusted, so you must pass your money test; you have to be able to give *and* receive freely. Be encouraged and allow the Holy Spirit to move in your finances so that you can be set free. God wants to get you out of debt, which is a miracle when He does.

When we were young, I could not see how God would get us out of debt because it seemed impossible, but He did it. We worked extra hard, cut out expensive extras, and took many steps on our own, and God came through with miracle after miracle. I believe that and am asking God to do that for you. Give God your finances and allow Him to advance the kingdom through your finances.

Give God your body and allow Him to heal it. It does not matter how impossible it looks or if your situation is stubborn and won't change. It does not matter that you are on medication. Continue to take it, but pray and ask God to show you what you can do and what He wants you to do and believe for supernatural healing in your body. God wants to touch your body and wants you to be pain-free; He wants you to move into supernatural healing. So let God influence you; I don't care how long it takes.

YOUR JOURNEY WITH GOD IS UNVEILED MORE AND MORE EVERY DAY

Let God talk to you. Feed on the Word of God for health in your body and believe that God will supernaturally deliver you from sickness and disease. Feed on the Word of God not only for healing but for finances as well. God can do it and can supernaturally keep you. God wants you to be healthy and pain-free; the Spirit of God is more than willing to do that.

With deliverance, in some situations, people do not understand or know why they are going through certain experiences. Evil spirits are in operation. They are being handed down and assigned through the bloodline. People inherit these and do not understand what has happened. These evil spirits are very tenacious and stubborn. You need to turn yourself over to the Lord in the holy fire and separate yourself so you can discern the workings of these familiar spirits.

You need to be the one that overthrows them and stops this from continuing in your family.

> *You can address these issues and break their power, and if you get pushback, you know you are making progress.*

I want to encourage you to turn your spiritual life over to the Lord so that you can get hot enough to know and discern what may be working against you. It is not your fault because these problems are common worldwide among people. But you have to take a stand against them even if you cannot see or understand what is happening. You can address these issues and break their power, and if you get pushback, you know you are making progress. You must also feed yourself on the Word of God, pray, and get hot enough so that you expose these demons.

You need to hand yourself over to God in the following areas: finances, health, regarding the demonic, and familiar spirits enforcing curses on generations through your bloodline. You hand your life over so that you can be strengthened to the point where you can come and stand against these powers working against you (Ephesians 6:12). When you turn yourself over to God in every area of your life, you will start to be delivered and healed and see the manifestation of the kingdom of God. I know this for a fact.

So many people do not understand why they are struggling. Then they hear the Word of God and experience some catalyst that causes them to act. Sometimes it is an encounter at a conference, reading a book, or praying and fasting. This catalyst causes them to see and take action, and then deliverance starts to break forth. The devil will begin to unravel, and he will no longer have a stronghold in that area of finances, healing, or deliverance. You start to encounter freedom. As you gain leverage, you can enforce that blessing instead of perpetuating the curse. Their ability to hold you diminishes.

The power of God rests in the name of Jesus. These demons shake and lose their control when confronted with the full authority in His name. Mention the name of Jesus in any area of your life where you want to see a breakthrough; invoke His name and authority daily. If any demonic spirits are involved in these areas, you will start to see a change in your finances, body, and spiritual life. You will start to see your finances break open. Your body will begin to heal, and you will see the bondages from these familiar spirits diminish. Invoke the name of Jesus, and pray in the Spirit. You are not perfect, but you are being transformed into what you are supposed to be. This journey is unveiled more and more every day.

Brethren, I do not count myself to have apprehended; but one thing I do, forgetting those things which are behind and reaching forward to those things which are ahead, I press toward the goal for the prize of the upward call of God in Christ Jesus. Therefore let us, as many as are mature, have this mind; and if in anything you think otherwise, God will reveal even this to you.

—Philippians 3:13–15

You are not striving to be perfect—it is God who is perfecting you. Paul said he did not claim to have arrived, but he pressed on toward the mark of that high calling, that perfection, even if he hadn't obtained it. Paul was always pressing on to the goal, which is what we are to do. I desire to see you get to the place where you do not fail, and you are not unproductive. Peter said that we are partakers of the divine nature, and if you add your faith to all these virtues—self-control, brotherly love, and kindness—and if you do all these things, they will help you be productive and never fail (2 Peter 1:4–8).

15

CHARACTER, PERSONALITY, AND ACCOUNTABILITY

Therefore, brethren, be even more diligent to make your
call and election sure, for if you do these things you will
never stumble.

—2 Peter 1:10

W e think of faith as so important because, without faith, we cannot please God (Hebrews 11:6). Much emphasis was placed on the gifts of the Spirit during the charismatic movement and then on faith in the Word of Faith movement. However, until now, in the body of Christ, we have not yet placed much emphasis on character, personality, and accountability; a focus on these qualities will increase in these last days.

But also for this very reason, giving all diligence, add to your faith virtue, to virtue knowledge, to knowledge self-control, to self-control perseverance, to perseverance godliness, to godliness brotherly kindness, and to brotherly kindness love. For if these things are yours and abound, you will be neither barren nor unfruitful in the knowledge of our Lord Jesus Christ. For he who lacks these things is shortsighted, even to blindness, and has forgotten that he was cleansed from his old sins. Therefore, brethren, be even more diligent to make your call and election sure, for if you do these things you will never stumble.

—2 Peter 1:5–10

GOD'S PERSONALITY MUST BECOME
OUR PERSONALITY

Peter says he wants you to add these things to your faith. Previous to this, Peter said that we are partakers of the divine nature because of the promises given to us (2 Peter 1:4). As a result of these promises, we are partakers of or partners with the divine nature. To be like God is profound to me. Ephesians says, "Therefore be imitators of God as dear children" (Ephesians 5:1). These virtues that we are supposed to add to our faith are a group of characteristics that are God's personality but become our personality.

One of the virtues that you are to add to your faith is knowledge. You may think, *I have great faith*, but Peter is saying add knowledge to that faith, so I will add some knowledge to my faith. Then he instructed us to add self-control, perseverance, godliness, brotherly kindness, and love. Peter explains that if you possess these characteristics, you will never be barren but fruitful in the knowledge of our Lord Jesus Christ. On the other hand, if you lack these virtues, you are short-sighted and even blind, forgetting that you have been cleansed from your past sins. So 2 Peter 1:10 admonishes us to be diligent to make our call and election sure. You will never fail if you heed this very important instruction.

> *I pray that you always feel the supernatural need for knowledge and continually seek and want to know more.*

It is so crucial in these last days to focus on character. We think of faith that can move mountains, but you have nothing if you do not have love (1 Corinthians 13:1–13). Peter begins with your faith and adds all these different steps, and the very last virtue he mentions is love. Another one of the steps he mentions is knowledge, and you can never know enough.

KNOWLEDGE

After I went through different colleges, courses, and training for various professions, I thought, *I don't know if I can handle any more.* I studied to be a commercial pilot, and after I took the tests, which lasted two days, I got my commercial pilot license. Afterward, I was so exhausted that I slept for thirty-two hours. After that, I didn't think I could learn anything else. That was years ago, in 1989, and now we are in 2023. I am learning more about jet airplanes now than ever, and I still don't feel like I know anything.

We will never know everything. People often do not even see the need for knowledge. Sometimes we need it, but we don't see it until, suddenly, a circumstance arises that exposes that need for understanding knowledge. Then we get it. We will always need to add knowledge to our faith. I pray that you always feel the supernatural need for knowledge and continually seek and want to know more. After you have knowledge and develop and mature, Peter says to add self-control to that.

SELF CONTROL

As you know more, experience more, and do more, you will have to have self-control. For me, it is about knowing when to step in and when not to; when to say something, and when not to. It is managing your words, thoughts, and actions. As you develop, get smarter, and are full of knowledge, you must have wisdom because you have to be able to control yourself and know when to speak and when to be quiet. You could offer someone advice when they are not asking for it, and they will not want it. You can see that person will get hurt and want to help them, but you can't help them. You have to know when to hold back and when to speak, which is all part of self-control.

PERSEVERANCE

To self-control, you must add perseverance; in other words, you must stay in there. Peter was saying that he wants you to always be in gear, never go into neutral, and never get lukewarm in the days we live. You must persevere and keep going, and you have to tell yourself that. Perseverance is constantly engaging God and being led by the Spirit. Then to that perseverance, you must add godliness.

GODLINESS

We are to be imitators of God as dearly loved children and be godly (Ephesians 5:1). We are like God because we are imitators of Him, and we are always to be thinking about that. What is godly? What would God do? What would Jesus do if He were here? Think about being in a certain situation and what you would say or do. I mostly think about what Jesus would do in that situation; I think about Scripture and start implementing and applying it.

> *You temper your actions by imitating what God, your Father, would do.*

After you have learned to persevere, then you add godliness to that. So you temper everything with this thought: *This is how I will act because it is appropriate and godly to act this way. I will not say this, and I will not do that.* You temper your actions by imitating what God, your Father, would do. You act like your Heavenly Father and imitate Him.

BROTHERLY KINDNESS

Peter says that to godliness, we are to add brotherly kindness. Even after you feel like you are getting closer to God and becoming more like Him, you must seek to be kind to people. You must be tolerant in the sense that you understand people's weaknesses. However, I am not saying that you excuse people's sins, but you are kind about it. You must be understanding of what they are going through. Put yourself in their situation and try to outwardly grace your words and actions with kindness. After brotherly kindness, Peter advises us to add love.

LOVE

Love is patient, love is kind. It does not envy, it does not boast, it is not proud. It does not dishonor others, it is not self-seeking, it is not easily angered, it keeps no record of wrongs. Love does not delight in evil but rejoices with the truth. It always protects, always trusts, always hopes, always perseveres.

1 Corinthians 13:4–7 NIV

Love is patient, and love is kind, and as you read through 1 Corinthians 13, you will see all the characteristics of love. If you walk in these virtues and do all these things, you have added to your faith and diligently made your call and election sure.

223

And now abide faith, hope, love, these three; but the greatest of these is love.

—1 Corinthians 13:13

The last school I attended before my doctorate was my two-year program, where I learned the most about faith and the Scriptures about being in Christ. I was built up strongly. However, I didn't find out until later that the greatest of these was love, not faith, as it says here in 1 Corinthians 13:13. Then I realized Peter was saying that you must add all these things *to* your faith, which had to do with your character. People were moving mountains with their faith and were seeing all these prayers answered, and it was an amazing time back then. Yet most of my friends are not even in ministry anymore.

SATAN CAN COME IN AND GET YOU OFF TRACK IN YOUR CHARACTER

If I go back and think about my time as an undergraduate, I have only met two out of the hundreds in my graduating class still in ministry. That does not mean more aren't in the ministry, but I only know of two people in the ministry to this day. And from the two-year program I attended after my undergrad, I only know two people who are still in the ministry and moving with God. I thought the students from this school would always be in ministry because they were very powerful individuals. The problem is that satan comes in, and he steals from people.

> *Therefore whoever hears these sayings of Mine, and does them, I will liken him to a wise man who built his house on the rock: and the rain descended, the floods came, and the winds blew and beat on that house; and it did not fall, for it was founded on the rock. But everyone who hears these sayings of Mine, and does not do them, will be like a foolish man who built his house on the sand: and the rain descended, the floods came, and the winds blew and beat on that house; and it fell. And great was its fall.*
>
> —Matthew 7:24–27

I find this very thing when I talk to the people who are no longer in ministry and investigate what is happening with them. They did not add all these virtues, which are character traits, to their faith. These virtues place you on a solid foundation so that your house cannot be washed away when the rains come because you are established and strong. I now realize just how important this was the whole time. When studying faith, different supernatural manifestations, and the gifts of the Spirit, we were so excited because we loved it when God used us; we loved to experience the other realm. Unfortunately, satan can come in and get us off track in our character.

> *I do not pray that You should take them out of the world, but that You should keep them from the evil one. They are not of the world, just as I am not of the world.*
>
> —John 17:15–16

BE DILIGENT TO MAKE YOUR CALL AND ELECTION SURE

> *Your eyes saw my substance, being yet unformed. And in Your book they all were written, the days fashioned for me, when as yet there were none of them.*
>
> —Psalm 139:16

We are in this world, but we are not of it, and while I am here, I want to be fortified, lasting to the end. I want to pass all my tests, and I want to stay in there. Jesus established every one of us in our books written in Heaven before we were ever born.

Each one of our days was written in a book before one of them came to pass, yet how many people actually end up fulfilling their destiny? I have seen so many people wash out and fail. I have seen problems come to people I know, and I never guessed that they would lose heart.

We must stay diligent, and if we add all these other virtues to our faith, Peter promises us that we will not be barren or unproductive and will not fail. We have all these promises set before us so that we do not forget we are cleansed from our past sins and are not blind. However, remember that Peter says Christians can be blind and forget they are cleansed from their past sins. Peter says something at the end of this verse in 2 Peter 1:10 that I have never heard talked about or taught, "Therefore, brethren, be even more diligent to make your call and election sure." So what is your call?

God calls people and essentially says, "This is what I have for you, and I am calling you to do it. I have a mission for you, and I am assigning you to it." We all have a calling that God has for us, which God wrote in a book before we were born. If God elected you, chose you, and called you, why did Peter say to do everything you can and be diligent to make that calling sure? Some people think that once saved, you are always saved, and others say you can lose your salvation, and there are many arguments for, against, and between these extremes.

> *Therefore I make known to you that no one speaking*
> *by the Spirit of God call Jesus accursed, and no one*
> *can say that Jesus is Lord except by the Holy Spirit.*
> —1 Corinthians 12:3

1 Corinthians 12:3 says that you cannot say by the Spirit of God that Jesus is cursed because the Spirit would never say that; you cannot do certain things if you are in Christ. If you are doing these things, you need to check to see if you are even in Christ. Paul addressed these kinds of matters in his letters. Similarly, Peter said we must be diligent in making our call and election sure. He is giving us the idea that we could fall away and be lost.

> *Do you not know that those who run in a race all run,*
> *but one receives the prize? Run in such a way that*
> *you may obtain it. And everyone who competes for*
> *the prize is temperate in all things. Now they do it to*
> *obtain a perishable crown, but we for an*
> *imperishable crown. Therefore I run thus: not with*
> *uncertainty. Thus I fight: not as one who beats the*
> *air. But I discipline my body and bring it into*

subjection, lest, when I have preached to others, I myself should become disqualified.

—1 Corinthians 9:24–27

Paul said that after he preached Christ, if he were to live in the flesh, being ruled by his body and not disciplining it and making it listen, he could be eliminated—thrown away—from the race. This saying is hard for some people to accept. This idea of adding these virtues to our faith and that if we do these things, we will never stumble and never fail means that if we do *not* do them, we *could* stumble and *could* fail. And it's the same with many other truths in the Word. So I would not want to test those boundaries and find out.

I know many wonderful people who were wonderful friends who are completely gone now. Either they died early, are out of the ministry, or are struggling now. They were good people who loved God and wanted to serve Him, but satan attacked and targeted them; they did not keep up their temperature spiritually. They did not do all the things we discussed on all these levels that are so important.

I added up every person I went to college with from both universities, which totaled about two thousand graduates. Almost two thousand people on the earth right now, including me, should be walking in what Jesus walked in. I can only name, on one hand, the people I know that are still operating in that from my graduating classes. As I said, there could be more I don't know of, but I should have heard about them.

I know one individual named Roger, who is in India, and from what I understand, he has started over five hundred churches. Roger was very humble, and we spent a lot of time together in college, talking and studying. He was the most amazing man and wasn't trying to be a bigwig or impress anyone.

Roger was sent from another country to college here in America. He fasted, prayed privately, and prayed with me. We sought God and talked about Him, and then Roger returned to his country and did it. He made his call and election sure. I also know another person who is a pastor, and he still believes the same way and continues to serve the Lord. So I know a couple of individuals that continued, but there are so few. That was not God's will at all.

THE GREATER WORKS

Most assuredly, I say to you, he who believes in Me, the works that I do he will do also; and greater works than these he will do, because I go to My Father.

—John 14:12

Jesus was very diligent. I think about what He said in John 14:12, that we would do the works that He did and even greater works. If Jesus were on the earth right now, He would remind us of what He said. When Jesus worked with the disciples, and they failed in doubt, unbelief, or fear, He would say, "How long will I be with you?" (Matthew 17:17). In other words, "I will not be with you very long, and if you don't catch on, how will you be able to carry out the will of the Father? I am training you and getting you ready because I am leaving." Jesus said, "I am going to the Father. So you will do what I am doing, but then you will do even greater works."

> *And they went out and preached everywhere, the Lord working with them and confirming the word through the accompanying signs. Amen.*
>
> —Mark 16:20

People argue about the works of Jesus. Some religious organizations are against speaking in tongues, laying hands on the sick, casting out devils, freeing people from bondages, and preaching that God wants to prosper you. They are against all of that, but that *is* the message of the gospel. These signs and wonders confirm that the Word of God is being preached. They follow those who believe. If the Word is preached and the believing ones do their job doing the works of Jesus, these signs will follow us. However, Jesus would want to coach us right now on the greater works.

231

What if a whole room of people were healed, received financial freedom, or were delivered from familiar spirits and curses? What if they were delivered from problems that are not of God and should have been taken care of but were not? Jesus would want to mention the number of those receiving miracles and the intensity of the manifestation. However, these religious organizations come against the whole idea of miracles, signs, and wonders because of self-interest. They say, "That is not for this dispensation. That all left with the apostles." It is easier to do that and come against people that believe that way and try to discredit them than manning up and saying, "This is what we should be experiencing."

I do not believe it is God's fault that we are not seeing the greater works or even any works at all. Jesus warned it would be this way; it is a perfect example that God's will is not always done on the earth as it should be. If God's will were done, we would see the works of Jesus in the church and in every believer and even greater works than that. The gates of hell would not prevail against the church.

God's will is *not* always done, yet He is not to blame. He has established His will and let us know what it is. He said we would go beyond faith by adding all these other virtues, characteristics, and personality traits. We will go to that higher level, and then we will not be unproductive and blind; we will not fail but finish our race.

> *Go therefore and make disciples of all the nations,*
> *baptizing them in the name of the Father and of the*
> *Son and of the Holy Spirit, teaching them to observe*
> *all things that I have commanded you; and lo, I am*
> *with you always, even to the end of the age." Amen.*
> —Matthew 28:19–20

> *Therefore bear fruits worthy of repentance, do not*
> *think to say to yourselves, 'We have Abraham as our*
> *father.' For I say to you that God is able to raise up*
> *children to Abraham from these stones. And even*
> *now the ax is laid to the root of the trees. Therefore*
> *every tree which does not bear good fruit is cut down*
> *and thrown into the fire.*
> —Matthew 3:8–10

God's will is that everyone hears the Word of God and produces fruit in keeping with repentance, and I believe that for you. I believe this teaching on holy fire has helped you and given you the proper perspective, and when we all get to Heaven, I will see the fruit that came from this course. I believe I will see all the people you touched and the amazing works of God displayed on the earth because you took what you were taught here. I believe that you will bear much fruit for the kingdom of God.

PRAYER

I thank You, Father, that many, many, many will come into the kingdom because of holy fire. I thank You for fulfilling Your heart in every student's life so that You would produce everything they need inside and outside their lives. Father, I pray that You would bring the finances, that You would bring all the provision that is needed in their bodies and their minds, and bring spiritual wisdom and revelation. I thank You for the finances and deliverance from every type of evil in their lives. In the name of Jesus. Amen.

God bless you.

Salvation Prayer

Lord God,
I confess that I am a sinner.
I confess that I need Your Son, Jesus.
Please forgive me in His name.
Lord Jesus, I believe You died for me and that
You are alive and listening to me now.
I now turn from my sins and welcome You into my heart.
Come and take control of my life.
Make me the kind of person You want me to be.
Now, fill me with Your Holy Spirit,
who will show me how to live for You.
I acknowledge You before men as my Savior and my Lord.
In Jesus's name. Amen.

If you prayed this prayer, please contact us at
info@kevinzadai.com for more information and materials.

We welcome you to join our network at Warriornotes.tv for access
to exclusive programming.

To enroll in our ministry school, go to:
www.Warriornotesschool.com.

**Visit www.KevinZadai.com for additional
ministry materials.**

About Dr. Kevin Zadai

Kevin Zadai, Th.D., was called to the ministry at the age of ten. He attended Central Bible College in Springfield, Missouri, where he received a Bachelor of Arts in theology. Later, he received training in missions at Rhema Bible College and a Th. D. at Primus University. Dr. Kevin L. Zadai is dedicated to training Christians to live and operate in two realms at once— the supernatural and the natural. At age 31, Kevin met Jesus, got a second chance at life, and received a revelation that he could not fail because it's all rigged in our favor! Kevin holds a commercial pilot license and is retired from Southwest Airlines after twenty-nine years as a flight attendant. Kevin is the founder and president of Warrior Notes School of Ministry. He and his lovely wife, Kathi, reside in New Orleans, Louisiana.

CHECK OUT OTHER WORKS ON THIS
SUBJECT BY DR. KEVIN ZADAI

Kevin has written over sixty books and study guides. Please see our website for a complete list of materials!

www.Kevinzadai.com

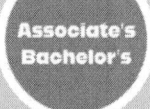